D1628017

WITHDRAWN

APPLIED SOCIOLOGY *for* SOCIAL WORK

LIVERPOOL JMU LIBRARY

3 1111 01512 5808

Sara Miller McCune founded SAGE Publishing in 1965 to support the dissemination of usable knowledge and educate a global community. SAGE publishes more than 1000 journals and over 800 new books each year, spanning a wide range of subject areas. Our growing selection of library products includes archives, data, case studies and video. SAGE remains majority owned by our founder and after her lifetime will become owned by a charitable trust that secures the company's continued independence.

Los Angeles | London | New Delhi | Singapore | Washington DC | Melbourne

APPLIED
SOCIOLOGY
for
SOCIAL WORK

EWAN INGLEBY

Los Angeles | London | New Delhi
Singapore | Washington DC | Melbourne

Los Angeles | London | New Delhi
Singapore | Washington DC | Melbourne

SAGE Publications Ltd
1 Oliver's Yard
55 City Road
London EC1Y 1SP

SAGE Publications Inc.
2455 Teller Road
Thousand Oaks, California 91320

SAGE Publications India Pvt Ltd
B 1/I 1 Mohan Cooperative Industrial Area
Mathura Road
New Delhi 110 044

SAGE Publications Asia-Pacific Pte Ltd
3 Church Street
#10-04 Samsung Hub
Singapore 049483

Editor: Kate Keers
Editorial assistant: Talulah Hall
Production editor: Katie Forsythe
Marketing manager: Camille Richmond
Cover design: Wendy Scott
Typeset by: C&M Digitals (P) Ltd, Chennai, India
Printed in the UK

© Ewan Ingleby 2018

First published 2018

Apart from any fair dealing for the purposes of research or private study, or criticism or review, as permitted under the Copyright, Designs and Patents Act, 1988, this publication may be reproduced, stored or transmitted in any form, or by any means, only with the prior permission in writing of the publishers, or in the case of reprographic reproduction, in accordance with the terms of licences issued by the Copyright Licensing Agency. Enquiries concerning reproduction outside those terms should be sent to the publishers.

Library of Congress Control Number: 2017941637

British Library Cataloguing in Publication data

A catalogue record for this book is available from the British Library

ISBN 978-1-4739-8439-4
ISBN 978-1-4739-8440-0 (pbk)

At SAGE we take sustainability seriously. Most of our products are printed in the UK using FSC papers and boards. When we print overseas we ensure sustainable papers are used as measured by the PREPS grading system. We undertake an annual audit to monitor our sustainability.

CONTENTS

ABOUT THE AUTHOR

Ewan Ingleby worked in residential social work in London during the 1990s. He went on to complete a PhD in Social Sciences and PGCE at Surrey University, and taught at New College Durham on the Social Work degree programme. Ewan was appointed as Senior Lectuter in Education at Teesside University in 2006 and he teaches on the Education Doctorate, the MA in Education, the University's PGCE (FE) and undergraduate education programmes.

Ewan was appointed as co-leader of Teesside University's 'Learning for the 21st Century' research challenge in 2017, in order to develop research in education across the university. He is an elected member of the International Committee of the International Professional Development Association (IPDA) and he has worked on research funded by the Higher Education Academy. Ewan has published research articles in peer-reviewed education journals and has participated in education conferences at national and international events.

ACKNOWLEDGEMENTS

Thank you to my friends, colleagues and students at Teesside University for your contribution to the debates and discussions that have helped to form this book. The book is based on the teaching, learning and professional development reflections of a number of academic staff who are associated with the university. Particular thanks go to Dr Clive Hedges at Teesside University and Dr Jonathan Tummons at Durham University, who have contributed to many of the discussions on the subjects covered in this book. Thank you also to Professor John Fulton of Surrey University and Professor John Davis of All Souls College, Oxford, for encouraging me to persevere in reconciling studying, research, writing, teaching and administration. As ever, I am particularly grateful for the support of my family, especially my wife Karen and my children Bernadette, Teresa and Michael. Without them, tomorrow would always be a much harder day.

Ewan Ingleby, 8 May 2017

CHAPTER 1

INTRODUCTION

SOCIOLOGY AND SOCIAL WORK

This book explores how sociology can be applied to social work. 'Sociology' and 'social workers' may be spoken about within the same sentence. They are strongly linked, and yet both sociology and social work are more complex than this. Sociology is an academic discipline with a profound philosophical heritage and social work is a complex profession. In the UK, social work has evolved to become a discipline that is characterised by a number of highly skilled professionals working in key areas to protect the rights of a complex range of individuals. This reflection outlines the need for this book. Sociology is a key discipline that social workers study, but the subject itself can be misinterpreted and its applicability can be lost in inaccurate understandings of the nature of the social work profession. Sociology is not a new subject. It is not a subject that is confined to the study of companionship. Sociology is a discipline that connects to the pursuits of philosophers who try to understand the world that they live in.

The book explores how three key sociological theories (functionalism, interactionism and conflict theory) can be applied to understanding the world frequented by many of the individuals who work with social workers. The book focuses on these three sociological perspectives because they reveal central concerns within the discipline of sociology. The concern with how social factors create social problems is at the heart of functionalism. Functionalists are interested in how the social world generates social meaning. 'Societies' are regarded as being more important than individuals. A 'macro' approach is taken in understanding the social world. This is similar to the questions that were pursued by philosophers like Plato (Audi 1999). Instead of focusing on individual perceptions, such philosophers pursue big questions. The nature of love in its entirety is considered. There is an attempt to explore the fundamental essence of love. There are also social workers who explore the answer to fundamental questions. The pursuit of how society shapes the plight of individuals is one example of such a big question. Social forces are regarded as being beyond individuals, in this instance.

A contrasting sociological perspective, interactionism, forms the basis of one of the other key themes in this book (Ingleby 2013). Interactionism is based on exploring the perceptions of individuals. As opposed to seeking causes to social factors that are beyond the understanding of individuals, the meaning generated by individuals becomes central to the social world. We witness what Audi (1999) refers to as a Copernican revolution of thought. Just as Copernicus was the scientist who discovered that the universe revolves around the sun, so, too, interactionists explore how individuals generate meaning through interaction. An interactionist might argue that there is no point in pursuing the answer to 'big questions' to which there are no answers. We can never identify the fundamental essence of 'love' in its entirety. We can, however, discover an answer to the questions asked of individuals. We can ask how it feels to be loved. In this way, the big question is turned around. It becomes a different question that is asked of an individual and there will be an answer. This way of exploring sociology is also at the centre of much social work. The perceptions of individuals are explored. 'How do you feel?' is a key question that is asked by social workers in general. This is why this second sociological perspective is central to the material in the book.

The third sociological model that is explored is known as 'conflict theory'. This concept is based on the writing of Karl Marx. In this sociological model, the implications of the material world are explored. Marx (2013) draws attention to the importance of economic forces with regards to their impact on the lives of individuals. It is of interest that there are aspects of conflict theory that are similar to functionalism. Classical Marxism places an emphasis on the wider economic forces that are beyond individuals in that they are regarded as transcending the person. Capitalism, as an economic system, predates this author and there is every likelihood that it will exist for many years to come. In classical Marxism, the economy is studied in a functionalist way. The economy is regarded as being greater than individuals. Part of the reason for conflict theory being regarded as a complex aspect of sociological theory is due to the other strand of thought that contributes towards Marxist theory. This 'neo-Marxist' thinking places an emphasis on the importance of individuals engaging with social structures and generating new meaning. This is similar to interactionism. Thinking, conscious individuals are not regarded as being distinct from economic forces. They engage with the social world and create meaning in profound ways. The advantage of this way of thinking about the social world connects to much social work practice. As opposed to viewing social factors as the cause of every social problem, there is an acceptance that individuals are also influential in creating a meaningful social world. Conflict theory is a useful sociological concept because it appears to embrace both strands of sociological thought. A sensible way of resolving this 'either/or' dilemma appears to rest in accepting that the social world is a combination of social and individual factors. This enables us to have an appropriate methodology for exploring the issues that are confronted by social workers.

BOOK STRUCTURE

The book is divided into a number of key chapters. The rationale of the book is based on my own experiences as a social worker working with children and young people with learning disabilities and challenging behaviour. I relied on understandings of sociology and psychology to help me with my practical work as a residential social worker. My understanding of the circumstances influencing these individuals was based on reflecting on the ideas of sociologists who are associated with functionalism, interactionism and conflict theory. Although I worked predominantly with children and young people, I also had some experiences in working with older people. Reflecting on these experiences has led to me writing a book that I would have liked to have accessed in my time as a social worker. The book is divided into a number of key chapters.

The first main chapter, Chapter 2, begins by identifying the key concepts and academics who are associated with functionalism (for example, Émile Durkheim and Talcott Parsons). Key concepts (for example, the analogy that social systems are like biological organisms) are outlined. After explaining the ideas within functionalism, the paradigm is analysed and appraised in order to help develop engagement with the material in the chapter. The final section of this chapter applies functionalism to social work. The chapter outlines that the emphasis on providing support from the state can be traced back to the functionalist emphasis on having a broad social focus. It introduces the important theme that wider social factors influence our work within social work, and that people are not simply dependent on their individual characteristics – they are influenced by social factors. Our work as social workers becomes more effective on considering the impact that these social factors have on the lives of those individuals and communities with whom we work.

Alongside accepting the importance of social factors, we also have to take into consideration the significance of individuals and how they influence the social world. This theme is explored in the second main chapter of the book, Chapter 3. The focus on individuals within society has been made famous by the German sociologist Max Weber. The understanding of individual perceptions can also be traced back to the philosophy of Immanuel Kant with his 'Copernican revolution of thought' that considers micro as opposed to macro questions. Individual perceptions are at the centre of interactionism. This concept is analysed by reflecting on the strengths and weaknesses of approaches that focus on individuals. The content of Chapter 3 then applies interactionism to social work. In Chapter 3, it is explained how policies that emphasise 'the rights of individuals' and 'personal responsibility' can be linked back to interactionism. A media perception of social work in the UK portrays social workers as being 'beyond reality'. The emphasis on the importance of individuals is beneficial because this complements explanations that are based on macro social factors. An advantage of interactionism rests with the exploration of individual factors. This sociological perspective identifies that there are individual circumstances influencing social problems and challenges. By studying interactionism, we become more aware of the nature of these challenges.

Chapter 4 considers the rationale behind Marxist understandings of the social world with their emphasis on the importance of the 'means of production'. The chapter outlines the complexity of classical Marxist and neo-Marxist understandings of the social world. The content presents an analysis of what has come to be known as 'conflict theory'. Marxism is then analysed by reflecting on its ideological and practical strengths and weaknesses, and this analysis is applied to social work by considering the advantages and disadvantages for social work of Marxist understandings of society. Many social problems are rooted in economic causes, and the negative consequences of poverty in communities can lead to all sorts of challenges for social workers. Marx recommends the creation of an egalitarian society. In this chapter, we consider whether or not such a social system will produce a world where social work is less necessary than in a capitalist social order.

Once the three sociological theories have been introduced, analysed and appraised, the content of the book moves on to reflect on key social groups with whom social workers engage. In Chapter 5, the concept of childhood is explored by considering sociological perceptions of childhood. The experience of childhood is considered through our three key sociological lenses (functionalism, interactionism and conflict theory). The chapter draws on cross-cultural comparisons of childhood in order to reveal the complexity of understandings of childhood in the human world. It is suggested that understanding the social creation of 'childhood' enables social workers to become reflexive. Concepts of childhood that have previously been regarded as being 'fixed' can be challenged and viewed differently.

Chapter 6 explores the sociological understandings of learning disabilities. The social, personal and economic consequences of learning disabilities are considered in the chapter. The merits of viewing learning disabilities as a form of social creation are outlined for social workers. Awareness of the sociology of learning disabilities enables social workers to challenge innate, fixed perceptions of learning disabilities as innate. The chapter reveals how inclusivity has become a key part of our approach to learning disabilities in the UK. This situation is produced through a combination of social, individual and economic factors that have influenced professional practice with learning disabilities in the UK. In exploring the social construction of learning disabilities, our practice can be enhanced as social workers.

The creation of 'mental illness' is explored in Chapter 7 by juxtaposing traditional and scientific definitions. The chapter draws on the work of Michel Foucault by considering that understandings of mental illness in time and space define it. There is no fixed consistent understanding of mental illness. Traditional societies can interpret mental illness as a form of divine (or diabolical) possession. Likewise, late modern societies can understand mental illness in a scientific or Hippocratic way. In the chapter, this social creation of mental illness is applied to social work. This blending together of functionalist, interactionist and conflict theorist understandings of mental illness reinforces the importance of applying combined theoretical perspectives in helping to understand the nature of the social work.

The final main chapter, Chapter 8, explores the social creation of old age. The perceived social benefits of older people vary according to cultural contexts. Traditional societies may associate old age with 'wisdom' and 'advantages' for society. Economic interpretations of 'age' may regard the older population as a 'drain on resources'. These differing understandings are social creations. The chapter explores the social conceptualisation of old age and its consequences for social work today.

BOOK PHILOSOPHY

The book reflects on the application of sociology to social work. In achieving this objective, each chapter has a particular structure so that the reader is guided through the content. When I teach academic modules, I like to structure the teaching sessions in a particular way. After introducing content, I enable the learners to analyse the material we are studying. When we analyse, we assess the strengths and weaknesses of key concepts. After identifying the central themes within each chapter, analysis is performed through reflecting on the strengths and weaknesses of the concepts that have been introduced. This analysis is supported with academic referencing. The final part of each chapter provides an overall appraisal of the concept. In appraising concepts, we assess the overall merits of the concept and make a summative judgement about its applicability. In order to provide overall synthesis of concepts, I like to provide the learners with some follow-up reading material. To exemplify how this works through the book, let us consider a social phenomenon that is related to sociology, social work and pedagogy: learning preferences. This learning initiative has interested academics since the turn of the century. The idea goes back to the work of a psychologist called Howard Gardner. It is proposed that there are many different ways of learning and that there are 'multiple intelligences'. Gardner identifies eight particular examples of intelligence (linguistic, mathematical, kinaesthetic, musical, natural, interpersonal, intrapersonal and visual intelligence). The sociological interest in this concept is revealed if we consider the social implications of Gardner's work for the academic curriculum. Gardner reveals that a narrow focus on numeracy and literacy prevents us from developing other forms of intelligence. A sociologist would be interested in how this produces consequences for social learning. A social worker would be interested in the consequences for children if the curriculum emphasis is placed on a narrow range of subjects. We could argue that those children who are excluded from school are less likely to be excluded if the curriculum is broadened to include other forms of intelligence. Why should visual intelligence and art be regarded as being less important than English, maths and science?

If I was teaching this topic, I would begin by contacting my students with some preliminary reading. I have recently written a blog for the British Educational Research Association (BERA), in which I reflect on the connection between economic structures and achievement levels in literacy. This is a way of introducing the students to the idea that our curriculum is influenced by a range of complex factors. In the formal teaching session, I would begin by identifying who Gardner is and what his ideas about multiple intelligences are. In the second part of the session, I would ask the students to analyse the strengths and weaknesses of the concept of multiple intelligences. A strength of Gardner's work is the realisation that there are a number of talents that need nurturing in learners. Any social worker who works with children with complex needs will support the idea of having as broad a curriculum as possible. A weakness of the Gardner argument is, however, the lack of intellectual rigour in the concept of multiple intelligences. Why eight forms of intelligence? Why not nine or ten or fifty and so on?! The final part of the teaching session, attempts at getting the students to make an overall judgement about the applicability of the concept of multiple intelligences. This ultimate judgement forms the basis of appraising content. At the end of the teaching session, I like to leave the students with some supportive reading about the topic. In the example that I have just presented, I use the comprehensive research study on learning preferences completed by Coffield et al. (2004).

The above example reveals the philosophy underpinning each chapter in this book: the content is introduced; analysis of central aspects of the concept ensues through consideration of its strengths and weaknesses; the appraisal assesses the overall merit of the idea. The final part of each chapter points the readers to supporting reading in order to consolidate further the learning process.

KEY INFLUENCES

In the book, I have been especially influenced by the philosophy of Kant and his argument that individuals understand the world they are in by drawing on their own unique interpretation of social phenomena. This makes me especially interested in the interpretations we all have of the social world. Ellingson (2009) uses the term 'crystallisation' in illuminating the idea that we are in the world and making sense of it. Just as the light passes through a crystal and transforms our understanding of light, so, too, do we make reality of the social world. In considering functionalism, interactionism and conflict theory, our social work practice can be enriched. Of course, sociology is a rich intellectual subject that is made up of a range of models of thought. The obvious question is: 'Why focus on three perspectives?' My answer is that the other perspectives in sociology are a hybrid of functionalism, interactionism and conflict theory. My other answer is that it is important to be able to understand what is in a book like this. I want the readers to be able to say that they understand what is in each chapter. By simplifying the focus to three key sociological perspectives, I am confident that you will enjoy the content in the subsequent chapters.

CHAPTER 2

FUNCTIONALISM AND SOCIAL WORK

INTRODUCTION

This chapter outlines how functionalism is useful for social workers. The chapter begins by describing what functionalism is and how it is applied to social work. Functionalism is then analysed by reflecting on its strengths and weaknesses. Functionalism is a paradigm or model of thought and, as such, it has academic strengths and weaknesses. To demonstrate academic skills, an overall appraisal of functionalism is given. Consideration is then given to how functionalism can be applied to our work with key groups of individuals. We explore how to apply functionalism to children, those with mental health needs or learning disabilities, and older people.

WHAT IS FUNCTIONALISM?

Functionalist sociologists, including Émile Durkheim and Talcott Parsons, may be portrayed as perceiving social groups to be more important than individuals (Ingleby 2013). Functionalism explores how social institutions (for example, 'the family' and 'the health system') work to make social groups function. The perspective assumes that societies, like biological organisms, have basic needs that must be met in order to survive. An example of such a 'need' is the importance of health. Functionalists consider that the social order is threatened if shared norms and values about health are not reinforced across social groups. These shared norms and values become widely accepted through socialising individuals, so functionalists are interested in studying the processes that are part of socialisation. Functionalist sociologists seek to identify the ways in which perceptions of health are then established and structured within social groups. One of the key functionalist thinkers is the French sociologist Durkheim. Durkheim's work is personified in the sociology of crime and punishment in classic social science texts such as *The Division of Labour in Society* (1893/1984), *The Two Laws of Penal Evolution* (1899–1900) and *Moral Education* (2002). The primary focus for Durkheim is not so much the individual but more the whole social body that is necessary in order to 'maintain inviolate the cohesion of society by sustaining the common conscience in all its rigour' (1893/1984, p63).

This way of visualising society results in an emphasis being placed on the social components that combine together so that a social group is given its definition. The institutions within a social group (for example, the family, the health system, the education system and political and religious institutions) become critically important in establishing a cohesive social group (Ingleby 2013). Functionalists are not just interested in social order. They also explore what causes disorder in social groups. The presence of social disorder reveals the complexity that exists within the social world. Taylor et al. (2004, p15) emphasises the importance of ensuring that we do not form a deterministic impression of social groups. It is possible to challenge the established order and this can lead to the expression of new forms of social behaviour. It is important to ensure that the social system is not exaggerated. This may result in a neglect of the importance of creative individuals who make choices and shape the social world in new and innovative ways. We will explore these themes further on in this chapter.

CASE STUDY

The three Halpin brothers came over to England from Eire in the 1950s. The brothers had no prospect of employment in Ireland and they saw England as a land of possibilities. The development of the welfare state was spoken about in Ireland with excitement. The brothers arrived in London via Paddington Station. They were amazed at the size of the railway station. It seemed bigger than the whole of their village. Although they were sad to leave their family in Ireland, the brothers noticed that England possessed an incredible infrastructure and they knew that they had made the right choice.

REFLECTIVE ACTIVITY 2.1

How is the case study useful for social workers?

FEEDBACK ON REFLECTIVE ACTIVITY

We can summarise the work of social workers by saying that they aim to meet the physical, intellectual, emotional and social needs of those with whom they work. It is interesting to reflect that the reason for which the 'Halpin brothers' have left Ireland is because they see England as having a much better infrastructure. If we live in a place where our needs are not going to be met, there is a huge incentive to leave. This is exactly what the Halpin brothers have decided to do. Regardless of who we are working with as social workers, it is essential to try to meet their physical, emotional and social needs. The case study reveals that particular cultural contexts (or wider social groups) are more successful in meeting the needs of others.

FUNCTIONALISM AND SOCIAL WORK

So far, we have defined functionalism as a sociological perspective that explores how social groups stay together and maintain consensus. This macro approach focuses on a bigger social picture by drawing attention to the importance of social institutions. The emphasis is placed on how social structures such as the education system, the health system and the political system are formed and how they work to benefit society. In this book, we make the point that, in the UK, there was relatively little statutory support offered to children and families prior to 1946. This pivotal date is the time when the welfare state became such an important part of UK social policy. William Beveridge's concept of a welfare state defeating 'five social evils' (disease, idleness, squalor, ignorance, want) was put into effect from 1946 onwards. The welfare state revealed itself in the form of a national health service for every UK citizen, a benefits system and state education. The acceptance that the wider social system impacted on the lives of children and families sounds very similar to functionalism.

It is important for social workers to become aware of how the social system impacts on the life chances of children and families. In general, in UK society, the welfare state is regarded in a positive way. We can argue that a concern with wider society links back to the work of the functionalists. We can also argue that it is important for social workers to become as fully aware as possible of the services from the welfare state that are available to help children, older people, those with mental health needs and those with physical or learning disabilities. It is important to acknowledge that life chances are influenced by social factors. This is emphasised by functionalists. This argument is exemplified if we reflect on the problems that are experienced by children and families who live in societies that do not have a welfare state. If the social system is underdeveloped so that individual families become accountable for their life chances, there are fewer opportunities for those children and families who are unable to look after their own interests (Ingleby 2013).

Functionalism can help social workers to realise how important it is to have robust social agencies that are able to plan for and coordinate effective health care and education. The welfare state has improved the life chances of many children and families, so it is essential to acknowledge the importance of wider social structures being able to help those who cannot help themselves (Ingleby 2013).

The following case study illustrates how the functionalist exploration of social systems can be applied to social work.

CASE STUDY

The Chua family lived in a rural part of eastern Malaysia for 15 years. Their experience of community was strong as the family lived in a village with other families. They formed a close community. The area of Malaysia they lived in had few amenities. Although the countryside was very beautiful and they had electricity and running water, the local infrastructure did not support a modern way of living. The roads were dirt tracks and the community could become isolated from the outside world in the rainy season in October. The Chua family decided to move from eastern Malaysia to Kuala Lumpur. They were attracted to the vibrant city, with its promise of a better infrastructure. The city appeared to be a fascinating combination of cultures as indigenous Malays, Chinese and Indian communities came together and worked together. The health and education system seemed so much better. It seemed as if the city could meet the family's every need. The Chuas knew that they had made the right choice in deciding to live in the city.

REFLECTIVE ACTIVITY 2.2

How can functionalism be applied to this case study?

FEEDBACK ON REFLECTIVE ACTIVITY

The Chua family are like many other families as they are trying to get the best quality of life they can find. Functionalist sociologists are interested in how different environments are more or less supportive for families. In this example, the city appears to be more supportive. The city provides the family with the key social services that are necessary for a good quality of life. There is a better infrastructure in the city compared with the isolation that the family may experience in the rainy season in rural eastern Malaysia. The sense of isolation or 'anomie' that is caused when the road network is flooded is one of the reasons why the family have moved into this more reliable infrastructure.

ANALYSIS OF FUNCTIONALISM AND SOCIAL WORK

In analysing functionalism, we are considering the strengths and weaknesses of this sociological perspective. Like all perspectives, or views on society, functionalism has strengths and weaknesses. The perspective looks at the 'big picture' (Ingleby 2013). We can argue that this is a strength of functionalism because attempts are being made to understand social organisations in their entirety. Moreover, functionalists explore how institutions work together to produce a cohesive social unit (Haralambos and Holborn 2008). The attempt to find answers to 'big questions' can be regarded as a noble pursuit. A number of famous philosophers (for example, Plato) have attempted to discover the answers to big questions. In exemplifying this point, Plato attempted to discover the fundamental essence of key aspects of the human world (for example, 'love'). The quest for these answers to key parts of the human world may be perceived as being the purpose of social science. Conversely, we can argue that a problem with pursuing the answers to big questions rests on the neglect of individuals (Ingleby 2013). Functionalists appear to be interested in wider social groups and their means of coming together and working together. This wide focus can result in the actions of individuals being neglected. As opposed to looking at the wider social unit, it is also important to take into consideration the impact of conscious individuals (Taylor et al. 2004). Some of the language used in functionalism appears to place too much emphasis on the social unit. The individual appears to become akin to Gilbert Ryle's likening to 'a ghost in the machine'. The individual person is almost disregarded (like a ghost) in favour of an emphasis being placed on the forces beyond the individual. Haralambos and Holborn (2008), Ingleby (2013) and Taylor et al. (2004) argue for the importance of a sense of balance. As opposed to focusing on wider social factors, it is important to emphasise the role of individuals as they shape social organisations. The realisation of this sense of balance is evident in the work of a number of anthropologists (for example, in the work of Ulf Hannerz, 1991). We see the application of neo-Weberianism as the emphasis on individual *verstehen* is applied in studies of society. 'Towns' and 'cities' do not just have a collective identity – these urban areas are formed by thinking and acting individuals. By focusing on the wider picture, we can miss individual detail, and this, in turn, can lead to a distortion of the social world. It is therefore important to have a sense of balance. There are social units that need to be studied if we are to understand society, and it is also important to realise that there are individuals who shape social units. A weakness with functionalism appears because the theory does not necessarily take the views of individuals into consideration (Haralambos and Holborn 2008; Ingleby 2013; Taylor et al. 2004). A social worker who focuses on entirely social factors in explaining social problems is accounting for only half of the explanation. There are wider social causes, but there are also individual factors and these individual factors need to be taken into consideration, alongside the social factors (Haralambos and Holborn 2008; Ingleby 2013; Taylor et al. 2004).

CASE STUDY

Petra was adopted at birth. Her adoptive parents had no idea of who her real parents were and had little knowledge of Petra's background. Petra lived in a very supportive household. Her adoptive parents were wealthy and Petra was given everything she could have asked for. She was introduced to other children in the hope that she would make friends. Petra's adoptive parents spoke to her in ways that attempted to develop her powers of speech, and they always tried to engage in conversation with Petra. Despite their demanding professional work (Petra's parents are both university lecturers) they made sure that they were always there for their daughter. They provided resources for Petra's education and appeared to be model parents. Once Petra started school, she began to struggle academically. No matter what was done for Petra, she found learning to be a challenge. Her parents tried everything. They paid for a private tutor to come to the house so that Petra could receive additional maths and English lessons. One of her father's academic friends admitted that he could not understand why it was that so much was being done to help Petra as it yielded little benefit for her academic progress.

REFLECTIVE ACTIVITY 2.3

What is of interest to social work and functionalism about this case study?

The case study reveals that everything is not determined by social factors. We see a child who is adopted by a couple and yet the girl is not what we might expect her to be. Petra is not academic, even though her parents are university lecturers. Petra does not excel where we would expect her to excel, in view of her family circumstances. We are presented with the impression of a child who is struggling to do well in a world she has been brought up in. The case study is interesting because the content reveals to us how we need to focus on factors that are beyond the social world. There are individual factors influencing children like Petra. No matter how much we choose to focus on the social world, there are idiosyncratic factors impacting on others and their circumstances. Some of these factors may link back to genetic inheritance. It seems that Petra may be more a product of 'nature' than 'nurture'. Perhaps she resembles her 'birth' parents? This reveals that the functionalist emphasis on the social world does not address all the important issues. As social workers, we must realise that social factors account for just part of the explanation of what is important in the human world. There are other influential components of the human world that are beyond what is social. This reveals that social work can only rely on functionalism for part of the explanation of the world. The explanation of the other part of the world that is not explained by social factors comes from alternative perspectives. As social workers, committed to holistic practice, we need to combine sets of ideas if we are to gain a realistic understanding of individuals and their circumstances.

APPRAISING FUNCTIONALISM

Every academic perspective has overall strengths and weaknesses. The functionalist approach, with its focus on 'social systems', may be perceived as making a mistake. There is an emphasis placed on the importance of the social system and this may result in the actions of individuals being neglected. The consequence appears to be an exaggeration of what is beyond the individual. It is, of course, important to draw attention to the 'wider picture', but it is also vital to acknowledge that individuals manipulate the social world in creative ways so that 'negotiated meanings' are produced (Lopez and Scott 2000, p17). As Lopez and Scott (ibid.) argue, individuals are 'far more differentiated from one another'. Social interaction is a result of both individual and social factors. The functionalist emphasis on a macro social order can neglect the actions of creative individuals (Ingleby 2013).

In appraising functionalism, we reflect on the overall contribution that this perspective makes to our work as social workers. We have seen in this chapter, thus far, how functionalism makes a positive contribution to social work practice. Despite the weaknesses in the perspective regarding the exaggeration that is placed on wider society, a strength of functionalism appears in the emphasis that is placed on the importance of the social world. Social workers are often supporters of the welfare state. We can argue that the concept of functionalism, with its focus on wider society, is influential in the emergence of a notion of state responsibility. Our work as social workers is influenced by an acceptance of the importance of engaging with wider society. It is in general viewed as being important for individuals to be 'less isolated' and 'more included' in social groups. We can, however, draw attention to the way in which ideas about society change. This can pose problems for our overall appraisal of the effectiveness of social work. Ideas are subject to change over time.

The popularity of ideas depends on a number of factors. Social, political and economic forces appear to influence the emergence of ideas at different times. This is commented on in the work of philosophers such as Foucault. In Foucault's work, there is reflection on how power changes in societies over time. Foucault's philosophy reveals that ideas about the social world are never static, and that they depend on a number of complex variables. If ideas are able to change over time, this suggests that the concept of the importance of having a wider society to nurture the individual will also vary over time. This appears to be the case, and is revealed in the concept of 'laissez-faire'.

Within this culture of individualism, there was no real provision by the state for services for individuals. It was only over time that this concept changed and we began to see the emergence of the acceptance of the importance of a welfare state. Ideas about society are also influenced by space as well as time. If we go to other parts of the world today, we see that the ideas that we accept as 'true' in general are disputed elsewhere. There are other cultural contexts (for example, parts of the USA), where there is not an acceptance of the idea that individuals should be looked after by wider society.

In this cultural view, it is perceived as being important for individuals to be self-reliant. This seems to be similar to the views of laissez-faire England.

In providing an overall appraisal of functionalism, we can argue that the idea is helpful as it draws attention to the importance of wider social structures. Much of our work as social workers involves meeting the needs of children, older people, those with mental health needs and those with physical or learning disabilities. A common strand that runs through our work with these client groups is a wish to integrate these social groups within wider society. It is not usual for us to seek to encourage an extreme form of individualism within these groups. This suggests that functionalism is an intellectual ally to our practice as social workers.

CASE STUDY

Alan is a retired social worker. He specialised in working within mental health. Alan reflected on how professional practice has changed in this area of social work. In the past, there was an emphasis placed on the institutionalisation of the mentally ill. Those with mental health needs were often removed from their communities and placed in institutions that were separate from the outside world. Alan said that many of his experiences when liaising with organisations like this were similar to the Ken Kesey (1962) novel *One Flew Over the Cuckoo's Nest*. As opposed to caring for those with mental health needs, the emphasis was placed on isolating individuals from the rest of society. Alan noted that the asylum system changed in the UK from the 1980s onwards as those with mental health needs were incorporated into the community. According to Alan, this happened because of a concern over money and budgets. It became expensive running the asylums so a new approach was introduced that led to 'community care'. Alan reflected that 'care in the community' was preferable in his view as the rights of individuals were being acknowledged.

REFLECTIVE ACTIVITY 2.4

What is of interest to social work and functionalism about this case study?

This case study highlights a difficulty that is inherent in placing too much emphasis on social factors. The asylum system resulted in the incarceration of those with mental health needs. Huge institutions were constructed in order to control and regulate those with mental health needs. The regulation of these 'patients' is an example of how a social group controlled and managed a health need. We see a classic example of social control, as a problem sector of society was removed and placed in institutions. Over time, we see a change in the treatment of those individuals with mental health needs. The asylums are closed down and a new way of working with those who have mental health needs is introduced. The asylum system reveals the negative consequences of placing too much emphasis on social regulation. If individuals are removed from their communities and placed in institutions, we can argue that their individual rights are being infringed. In this example, those with mental health needs are not being respected. There is no awareness of the importance of the individual. Ideally, we should nurture a system that is characterised by awareness of individuals and social responsibility. If functionalism can be used as a means of developing this point, it makes a positive contribution to our society. Too often, in functionalism, there can be an overemphasis placed on the social world. If the perspective is to be useful, then there should be a balance in emphasis. Social and individual factors are both important.

FUNCTIONALISM AND CHILDREN

Functionalism can help us in our work with children as the perspective draws attention to the importance of social construction. Childhood is socially made. There is, of course, a biological reality to childhood, a link to biological maturation, but there are also important social elements to childhood. Sociologists of childhood have revealed that certain categories of human societies are social constructions. In particular, it is revealed that adolescence and 'teenage culture' is socially made. In the UK and in the USA, there is a social construction of adolescence. A culture is associated with adolescence, clothes, music and appearance. The importance of this revelation helps us to see how the world can be socially constructed. Some of this social construction is positive, whereas other aspects of this socially constructed world can be highly negative. There are elements of teenage subculture that can be immensely destructive, for instance substance abuse can result in whole communities becoming dysfunctional. Functionalists have the power to show us that the social construction of identity holds possibilities for us. We can construct communities in ways that are positive or conversely make our social world extremely negative. Some of the interventions that are possible for social workers are based on this construction of the world. Rogerian therapy, with its emphasis on removing what are referred to as 'would/should dilemmas', is an example of an intervention that is based on social construction. Rogers (2004) argues that anxiety is a product of a would/should dilemma. The individual wishes to achieve something but they are unable to realise this wish, and the consequence is anxiety. Rogers argues that if we are to remove anxiety in individuals, we need to resolve the would/should dilemmas that are being experienced. The benefit of this way of working for us as social workers is that we come to realise that so much of the world is socially constructed. This is an advantage of functionalism. If we specialise in working with children and we realise that key aspects of their world are socially constructed, we can see that our interventions as social workers have the potential to make a difference. It is important to ensure that we make a connection with the people we are working with. If we are to become an effective role model for children, we need to make an emotional connection with them. This is when children are more likely to listen to the guidance we give them. Many of our successful experiences in working with children in residential care are based on this important principle. This example shows that social processes can help in our work with children as social workers.

CASE STUDY

James has always done moderately well at his academic work as a teenager. He is frequently reminded by his parents that he won a number of prizes for academic achievement when he was younger. From the age of 13 to 16 years, James seemed to be almost 'invisible' as he was never at either the top or the bottom of the class. Suddenly, something happened! James seemed to develop a skill and an intensity to his academic work. This seemed to coincide with his developing friendship with Michael and David. The three friends appeared to spend most of their time together. All three friends began to do well academically. They discussed politics and philosophy beyond their school lessons. Their marks in assessments and exams went from being in the middle range up towards the top of the class.

REFLECTIVE ACTIVITY 2.5

What is of interest to functionalism and social work about this case study?

In this example, we see how social processes influence the academic performance of individuals. The three friends in the case study come together and form an emotional bond. Their heightened social interaction influences educational performance, and this reveals the power of the social group. A combination of individuals is able to make a difference when they work together effectively. This is of importance for social workers as we are able to see the significance of social interaction in children's growth and development, however it is naïve to assume that simply placing a child with a particular group of children is beneficial. The case study shows that once a group of children make an emotional connection with each other, they are capable of producing social change. A 'dynamic' emerges that can work in either positive or negative ways. The example in the case study is positive, but there are other examples that are less positive. A child may make an emotional connection with groups of children who do not produce a positive social dynamic, and this may result in all sorts of social problems.

In contrast to the example in the case study, the child may become increasingly opposed to the social order as they are influenced in a negative way by their peers. Again, it is important to realise that it is not so much the individuals that the child is interacting with that is the critical factor. What becomes critical is the emotional con-nection being made by the individuals in this group. If we become aware of dynamics like this in our professional practice as social workers, our work can only be helped. We are able to understand why some children develop in ways that are relatively uncomplicated whereas other children are influenced in profound ways. The power of the social group is a particularly important aspect of human interaction. If we become empowered and see how these dynamics influence children, we are placed in a position to know when to intervene and when to stand back. This is like the idiom 'fools rush in where angels fear to tread'. To stand back and not rush in requires the perception to know that the group dynamic is working well. We can become more aware of this way of working by studying functionalism.

FUNCTIONALISM AND MENTAL HEALTH

Mental health is of interest to functionalism, and this academic perspective is able to help us in our work as social workers. Functionalists are interested in the social construction of health and illness. We see in this book that there are sociologists of illness who align themselves to functionalism. The explanation given for mental illnesses is social – the 'condition' is regarded as being a social construction. The argument runs that mental illnesses are actually nothing other than unexplained forms of deviance. Behaviour that cannot be explained is regarded as being 'men-tal illness' because it does not appear to fit into any of the other categories of deviant behaviour. This emphasis moves away from focusing on biological causa-tion and puts social construction at the centre of this explanation of mental illness. The advantage of this interpretation of mental illness for us as social workers rests in the challenge that is provided to the medical model. It may be assumed that this medical model is inevitably right, and that mental illnesses are assumed to have a biological cause if the medical model is applied in understanding mental illness. A challenge to this way of thinking can help those we are working with.

We will also see in this book how complex human physiology is. If we start interfering with the body's chemical balance, all sorts of unpleasant consequences can result, yet this is exactly what has happened in some of the treatment of the mentally ill. An assumption is made that the behaviour is a product of an aber-ration of the mind. A further assumption is made that this challenging behaviour can be rectified through a medical intervention. Both of these assumptions have the capacity to cause incredible harm to individuals. If someone is assumed to be 'mentally ill' and then given medication, this may produce a series of life-changing difficulties. Critics of electroconvulsive therapy (ECT) argue that there is no conclu-sive evidence that giving individuals who are 'mentally ill' electric shocks is of any benefit. Perhaps the individuals adjust their behaviour, precisely because they do not enjoy the experience of having electric shocks? This change in behaviour is therefore based on a punitive principle as opposed to being based on medical reasoning and science. If we explore the social causation of behaviour, we are essentially doing what functionalists recommend that we do. The emphasis is placed on social factors and a challenge is provided to the assumption that the medical model is capable of explaining health and illness. In this way, functionalism enriches our work with people suffering from mental illness. It becomes possible to regard those with mental health needs as individuals who are in need of our help, our support and, above everything else, our professional expertise.

CASE STUDY

When Tony was aged 79 years, he went on holiday with his wife to the Mediterranean. During the holiday, Tony had a number of episodes of breathlessness. He found it difficult to cope during these episodes so he went to the doctor as soon as he arrived home in England. The doctor explained to Tony that he was experiencing symptoms of heart failure, and Tony was prescribed medication that helped his condition. As Tony's heart was not working properly, his body was retaining fluid, and this was causing him to have 'panic attacks'. Tony was placed on a series of anti-anxiety drugs but this seemed to make his state of mind worse. He began to say whatever came into his mind in public. This was deeply unsettling for Tony's family.

REFLECTIVE ACTIVITY 2.6

What is of interest to functionalism and social work about this case study?

The case study shows a difficulty with the medical model of the world, and it confirms the importance of the functionalist emphasis on the wider social world in explaining social occurrences. In Tony's case, his treatment is provided by a 'modern' medical system that applies drug therapy to rectify illnesses. It is assumed that Tony's anxiety can be cured by medicine. This care comes from a scientific medical system, however the care that is provided is not necessarily correct. This care is provided because of the social acceptance that this is the correct way to treat illnesses. It is interesting that, in fact, the care that Tony receives makes his state of mind worse and not better. Tony's anxieties ease, but his state of mind results in his behaviour deteriorating.

As social workers, we need to ensure that we do not simply accept views that are dominant. Tony has experienced heart failure and this appears to be influencing his mental health. It does not appear to be the case that Tony's health can be completely regulated by medicine. This social understanding of health and illness does not appear to be working with Tony. If you were Tony's social worker, it might be better to recommend a form of treatment that is not based entirely on drug therapy, as the assumption that giving Tony 'medication A' will result in 'behaviour B' does not appear to be the case with Tony. The benefit of functionalism is that this sociological theory enables us to become sceptical of the medical model. We are able to become reflexive thinkers who can question the authenticity of the world we are living in. In this way, our professional practice can become more successful. Perhaps Tony can be treated in a way that is 'alternative'? Tony's anxieties may ease if he is enabled to have more contact with his family and friends. If this strategy is combined with drug therapy, we are then providing a more holistic type of treatment for Tony. We are able to become aware of this way of working by studying functionalism. The advantage of functionalism is that we can visualise the human world as a series of social systems. No single social system is correct – there are just different interpretations of what is happening in the human world.

FUNCTIONALISM AND OLDER PEOPLE

Functionalist sociologists are interested in how social systems are used to generate meaning and understanding. Ageing is a biological process and it is also an example of social construction. The meaning that is given to old age varies according to social systems. There are some societies that are respectful of ageing. Older people may be regarded as 'wise' and as making a positive contribution to society. There are other societies where there is a different view of older people. In these social groups, older people are not treated in ways that are positive, and we see the creation of stereotypes that emphasise the weaknesses of these older people. Functionalist sociologists are interested in the age at which these definitions are being applied. Although the biological processes of ageing are consistent, the social interpretations of age are not consistent. In the UK, there are increasing numbers of older people as our affluent society has enabled life longevity.

This can mean that older people are regarded as being 'a problem' for society or 'a drain on resources'. The way that older people are perceived is therefore a social construction. The negative portrayal of older people can be regarded as being an example of a social stereotype. It is assumed that all older people share the same qualities and characteristics, and, as social workers, it is important for us to challenge social stereotypes. It is not true that every older person causes problems for our society, indeed there are many older people who are an asset to the society in which they live. These older people can bring wisdom and experience to their society. If we realise that perceptions of the world are actually social creations, this can help us to try to make our social world a positive place. It is not true that 'all older people talk too much', however it is true that there are many older people who are lonely and isolated, and this may be why they enjoy talking when they are in company.

In the UK, the legacy of William Beveridge has led to the welfare state, and this social creation is responsible for the welfare of older people. Beveridge wanted the UK to become 'a new Jerusalem' – he was committed to removing what were described as 'social evils'. The social evils of 'disease, idleness, squalor, illness and want' all impact on the quality of life of older people. The creation of the welfare state has helped older people in the UK to have an improved quality of life. Functionalist sociologists are, therefore, able to show that changing social circumstances result in a direct improvement in the life of older people.

CASE STUDY

Mary is 80 years old. She is in quite good health and she lives with her husband, who is aged 79. Mary is critical of the way in which older people are portrayed by the media. It is as if all older people are in poor health and vulnerable. Mary and her husband have a very good quality of life. They go out every day and they do not rely on others to do things for them. Mary and her husband are very independent. When they went to a Christmas party with their son and his family, there was a dancing competition. Mary won the prize as the 'best dancer'. Mary laughed with her family and exclaimed: 'Who would believe it?!'

REFLECTIVE ACTIVITY 2.7

What is of interest to functionalism and social work about this case study?

The case study shows how societies create impressions about categories of people that are not necessarily true. There are always exceptions to the rule. It is assumed that older people are physically frail and that they are not able to do what younger people can do. In the case study, Mary is the 'best dancer' at a Christmas party. The case study shows that it is important that we do not act on stereotypes. These stereotypes are social creations, and not an accurate portrayal of the world in which we live. If the reality about older people can be manufactured in this way, by social interpretations, this allows us to become aware of the power of social construction. A perception of older people can be created that is either positive or negative, and the ingredients that form this perception of older people come from a complex set of sources. The media can be particularly influential. The French philosopher Jean Baudrillard (1983a/1983b) reflects on the creation of meaning in Western societies and he problematises 'the real' in these societies. The argument runs that there are various examples of what is real. Being an older person in England is a real experience. There are, however, distortions of reality, for instance a diary account from an older person is not the same as being an older person. There is, nonetheless, a blurring of what is real and what is not real. An architect's design of an older person's home and the actual building are two representations of what is real. In this instance, the boundary between what is real and what is not real is more blurred. Baudrillard also argues that we experience what he phrases as 'hyperreality'. There are examples where the model precedes reality: with older people, there can be the view that 'all older people are in poor health'. This stereotype is also a simulation of reality. It is an example of hyperreality.

FUNCTIONALISM AND LEARNING DISABILITIES

Functionalism is useful for us if we are working with people with learning disabilities. This sociological perspective allows us to be critical of the Western medical model. We have already seen in the book that the Western medical model interprets the world in particular ways. The philosopher Robin Downie (2000) makes reference to the importance of Hippocrates in explaining the philosophy that underpins the Western medical model, where it is assumed that 'condition A' can be 'cured' if 'treatment B' is applied to the condition. Downie argues that this perception of the world is problematic, and that there are many examples where it is not possible to provide a 'cure' in this way. The model that Downie prefers places an emphasis on 'healing'. Within healing processes, the emphasis is not placed on a 'magical cure'. The individual improves through interacting with others in ways that are therapeutic. Downie's ideas emphasise the importance of social construction. The philosophy rests on the important argument that we construct meaning and understanding in our social worlds. The advantage for us as social workers working with those who have learning disabilities can be seen if we try to apply the medical model in understanding learning disabilities. There is no 'treatment' that can be administered to make the 'condition' go away. Learning disabilities are forms of behaviour that are interpreted in particular ways. Autism, for example, is a state of mind, but there is not a medical cure for autism. The medical model creates categories of 'conditions' where there are universal symptoms, however it is difficult to do this with learning disabilities. Those who are suffering from medical conditions usually demonstrate a consistent set of symptoms, and this is not necessarily the case with learning disabilities. With autism, there are different levels of this particular learning disability, and some individuals have a milder form of autism than others. Autism does not result in an inability to function in society in all cases. Some people are referred to as 'being at the higher functioning end of the spectrum'. This complexity reveals that the social construction of learning disabilities is most significant. When we become aware that this social construction of meaning occurs in societies, we can become more flexible in our approach as social workers. We are in a position to question whether or not shared social understandings are examples of hegemony. This term, associated with Antonio Gramsci, a significant social thinker who has informed social theory, explains how dominant understandings appear in societies (Forgacs, 2014). The dominant understandings are often reinforced by the elite groups in society. These understandings become shared so that they form part of the dominant discourse about particular groups in society. In medieval England, those with learning disabilities were regarded as being punished by God for transgressions against the divine order. Functionalism can help us to realise that this is a social construction of the real world.

CASE STUDY

Amanda has learning disabilities and mental health problems. Amanda was not able to learn to read and she struggled with academic work in school because of her learning disabilities. Her 'frustration' at not being able to achieve what she wanted to do could lead to violent outbursts and feelings of paranoia. Amanda's parents watched a documentary about how those with mental illnesses had been treated in the past. Amanda's parents were shocked at how so many 'needy' and 'vulnerable' individuals were placed in asylums that were removed from mainstream society. It seemed to be so inhumane! It was explained to Amanda's parents that this occurred because of a perception of learning disability that existed in society at the time. Moral associations were made between learning disabilities and 'evil'. It was assumed to be the case that those with learning disabilities were being punished by divine powers.

REFLECTIVE ACTIVITY 2.8

How can functionalism help us to understand this case study?

In this chapter, we have argued that functionalists are useful because they draw attention to the importance of social construction. Understandings of learning disabilities are constructed by social groups. In the case study, Amanda has a combination of learning disabilities and mental health needs. The 'shock' expressed by Amanda's parents relates to the way in which these 'ways of being' were interpreted in the past. Urban (2009) uses the phrase 'ways of being' and 'ways of knowing' to highlight the importance of ensuring that policy and practice links together. The argument runs that we will only have effective services for children and families when policy and practice combine together. When Amanda's parents were looking back at past practices, we see an example of a separation of policy and practice. The policies towards those with learning disabilities were not being informed by 'sound' professional practice. In the case study, learning disabilities are being interpreted in religious ways. Urban (ibid.) argues that this separation of policy and practice can be rectified when we experience evidence-based practice. We need to ensure that the correct social circumstances are in place if this is to happen effectively. In the UK, there has been much emphasis placed on ensuring that those with learning disabilities are treated with dignity and respect. This is now a key part of our approach to embracing diversity. 'Learning disabilities' as a term has replaced 'handicapped'. We attempt to ensure that we are as enabling as possible as opposed to discriminating against those with learning disabilities. The social circumstances have now been produced in UK society that enable us to acknowledge that previous approaches to those with learning disabilities were wrong. Functionalists are interested in this example of how changing social circumstances have influenced interpretations of groups in societies. As social workers, we can become aware of this 'good practice'. The inclusive approach of societies such as the UK can be considered as an example of best practice. We can become aware of this good practice working with those with learning disabilities as a result of the ideas of the functionalists.

CONCLUSION

This chapter has explored how functionalism can be applied to social work. We have argued that so many social forms are socially constructed, and that different societies at different times have different interpretations of the social world. There is not a rigid acceptance of what is right and what is wrong in the social world. Functionalism draws attention to what is socially constructed in societies like the UK. This helps our practice as social workers across a range of social groups. The chapter has outlined the strengths and weaknesses of functionalism. We have argued that it is important to maintain a sense of reasonable focus, and that it is not right to emphasise the social world to the detriment of individuals who shape social structures. Social interpretations are important, but the social world combines with individual factors. It is important to see the connection between social circumstances and the work of social workers. The welfare state is a social construction, and this socially created welfare state has influenced all the categories of society that social workers are associated. It is a social creation that has made such a difference to the lives of children; older people; those with mental health needs and those with learning disabilities.

If we reflect on our own lives, we will probably realise that everything that has happened to us is a combination of individual and social factors. We are not just 'social animals' – we are biological organisms who are independent. However, we have a capacity to act in social ways. Our human social ways have produced some incredibly amazing aspects of society: our literary, musical and artistic expressions are fundamentally social. These expressions of social interaction are of interest to functionalists. Our work as social workers should not occur in isolation and functionalism can appear to be a natural ally to this. Of all the sociological perspectives, functionalism is arguably the most relevant to our professional practice. Political and economic ideas that are not helpful for our professional practice as social workers can be critiqued. This understanding of the social world can be critiqued and placed into perspective. The medical model has had its successes but we also see that it cannot explain everything. A healthy dose of functionalist scepticism can enhance our professional practice and make us better social workers.

CHAPTER 3

INTERACTIONISM AND SOCIAL WORK

INTERACTIONISM

Interactionists such as Max Weber draw attention to how individuals interact with each other. Weberian theory is an appealing lens through which to view social work. The word *verstehen* means 'understanding': the implication is that the individual ought to be the primary focus of investigation, and this links to much of the 'client-centred' practice that characterises social work.

Whitehead (2010, p6) is one of a number of social scientists who argues that Weber's concept of *verstehen* can be combined with his analysis of bureaucracy to give a powerful insight into the nature of UK society. Weber (1968) defines the word 'bureaucracy' as the 'rule by officials within organisations'. He associates bureaucracy with precision, continuity, discipline, strictness and reliability (Ingleby 2013), and argues that bureaucracy is a consequence of the Enlightenment and the subsequent emphasis that was placed on the importance of rationality and efficiency. Allbrow (1970, p47) notes that one of Weber's concerns was that bureaucracy would expand at such a rate that it 'controlled the policy and action of the organisation it was supposed to serve'. Weber (1968) provides an interesting analysis of bureaucracy: 'bureaucracy can be understood as being a specialised division of labour where different individuals are responsible for specialised tasks in achieving organisational goals' (Whitehead, 2010, p6). He developed the view that modern capitalist societies are characterised by a trend towards rationalisation. Whitehead (2010, p6) refers to this process as 'planned, technical, calculable and efficient processes' that are devoid of emotion.

In some respects, interactionism appears to be the opposite of functionalism. Taylor et al. (2004, p17) propose that within interactionism an emphasis is placed on negotiating meanings. Individual human encounters are not considered to be 'fixed' – they are regarded as being dependent on the negotiation of those individuals involved in the encounter. Whereas functionalists such as Durkheim place an emphasis on the importance of the social system, interactionists are associated with negotiating meanings that arise during social interaction. These encounters are regarded as being creative because individual human actors engage with the social world in an inventive way.

Interactionism is a sociological theory that aligns itself with 'symbolic interactionism'. This sociological perspective emphasises the importance of using symbols within human interaction. Speech is regarded as being a particularly important means for making sense of interaction, although Taylor et al. (2004, p17) are critical of what they phrase as the 'small-scale' nature of interactionism. It is difficult to generalise when the emphasis is placed on individuals, and the larger, wider social trends are not necessarily taken into consideration. Interactionist studies may therefore be seen as impressionistic and local, and unable to identify globally significant findings.

REFLECTIVE ACTIVITY 3.1

In your own personal development, do you think that you are a product of a social system or do you think that your personality is critically determined by yourself?

FEEDBACK ON REFLECTIVE ACTIVITY

An obvious answer to this question is that everyone is a combination of social and individual characteristics. It is problematic to say that you have been shaped entirely by 'the social world'. It is also problematic to argue that 'unique' personal characteristics are responsible for shaping every person – we are a mix of characteristics. This reveals the difficulties of being either 'for' functionalism or being 'against' interactionism. We can become placed in a complicated situation where we develop a form of 'tunnel vision', and can be blinkered to a particular view. This is a less than helpful way of understanding the social world.

INTERACTIONISM AND SOCIAL WORK

In contrast to functionalism, the interactionist school of thought emphasises the importance of individuals. In some ways, the two perspectives can be seen as being opposites. There is less focus on macro sociological structures, and more attention is given to the ways in which individuals negotiate meanings when they are taking part in social encounters. This sociological perspective is important for social workers because it reinforces the importance of meeting the individual needs of those we work with. The interactionist approach to social work endorses examples of professional practice that treat children as individuals, with the potential to grow and develop as long as this opportunity is presented to them. The word 'sociology' can be interpreted as emphasising the importance of studying groups of people, as the Latin word *socius* means 'comrade' or 'ally'. The meanings that are negotiated by social actors in, at times, impressionistic ways are not always automatically associated with sociology. If we apply the analogy of 'a forest' in helping to understand interactionism, the main focus of the interactionists is on the 'individual trees'. This interactionist approach can help us to realise the importance of meeting the needs of children and families in our professional practice as social workers. Interactionists are interested in exploring how individuals explore the social world and how meanings are generated in social contexts. The individual rights of children that are emphasised as being so important (Parton 2005) emerge as key in our work as social workers if we follow the philosophy of this perspective. If we adopt this interactionist approach, we are more likely to encourage the creativity of children and families, and we are, in turn, more likely to be 'small-scale' and impressionistic in our approach to working with children and families.

CASE STUDY

Maria wants to be a social worker who specialises in working with children. She is interested in how play can help children to grow and develop, and is aware of how 'free', or unstructured, play is used successfully in Sweden. During her social work degree, Maria came to realise that the education system in the UK places an emphasis on children achieving literacy and numeracy targets. In contrast, in Sweden, more emphasis is placed on children learning at their own pace, and meeting targets and achieving goals does not appear to be as important. Maria wishes we could have an education system that focuses on nurturing the creativity of individual children.

REFLECTIVE ACTIVITY 3.2

How can interactionism be applied to this case study?

FEEDBACK ON REFLECTIVE ACTIVITY

In the previous chapter, we saw that functionalists believe in emphasising the wider picture. They pay less attention to individual needs. The unfortunate consequence of this approach to social work can result in the needs of individuals being neglected.

In the UK, we hear discussions about a 'national curriculum' and meeting 'national targets' in education, which can result in the individual needs of children being neglected. Maria has experienced a different cultural approach to education that sounds more like interactionism as an emphasis is being placed on meeting the needs of individuals.

APPRAISING INTERACTIONISM

We have reflected on the strengths of the interactionist focus on negotiating meaning, but it is also important to acknowledge that there are weaknesses with interactionism. As opposed to overemphasising the strengths of interactionism for social work, we need to realise that there are problems in focusing too much on individuals to the detriment of the social system. This argument is supported by Lopez and Scott (2000, p29) when they reflect that, although 'individual minds' are important in holding 'knowledge', this knowledge is not isolated but is 'shared by those who interact together'. This is similar to the argument of Davis (1948, p87), who considers that 'social positions are matters of reciprocal expectation and must be publicly and commonly perceived by everyone in the group'. It is particularly important to acknowledge the role that others play in generating social meaning, as the interactionist emphasis on individuals can lead to a loss of focus on the rest of 'the social group'. A further criticism of interactionism concerns the implication that individuals are 'all important'. This sounds similar to Margaret Thatcher's comment that: 'there is no such thing as society. There are individual men and women and there are families.' This emphasis on the individual can come at the expense of neglecting the importance of the social system. It is an idea that goes against many aspects of good practice within social work, and can lead to a lack of significance being placed on the role that the social system has in helping to nurture and develop children.

CASE STUDY

Jill works in children's social services. She has noticed that, in recent years, more and more emphasis appears to have been placed on the importance of individual children. Jill recently worked with a child who was on the verge of being excluded from his primary school. Jill said that she was particularly shocked on one occasion when the child exclaimed: 'I can do anything in school!'. Jill thought this was an example of where too much attention had been given to the individual rights of the child. In Jill's day, the teacher was regarded as 'a sage on the stage'. This sense of respect and 'awe' seemed to be missing in school children today in general, according to Jill. She thought that this focus on the individual was not necessarily good, and could result in a sense of selfishness

(Continued)

(Continued)

and a preoccupation with the individual. Perhaps there ought to be more of an emphasis on what is beyond the individual? Jill wondered if more could be made of 'community' and the factors that hold communities together.

REFLECTIVE ACTIVITY 3.3

What is of interest to social work and interactionism about this case study?

The case study draws attention to the difficulties that can follow if we place too much emphasis on the importance of the individual, such as losing sight of social structures. Much of our good practice as social workers comes from having a welfare state that is based on the important principle of ensuring that as any people as possible are looked after as thoroughly as possible. The ideology behind the establishment of the welfare state places significance on social collectivism. The welfare state was a reaction against the individualism that characterised previous forms of health and social care that were in existence in the UK prior to 1946. The 'laissez-faire' governments that had previously governed the country embraced individualism, and the state left its citizens to look after their own interests. The principle was that the state ought not to intervene; however, centuries of individualism appeared to result in a number of social problems that were highlighted and described as 'social evils' by Beveridge: 'disease, idleness, squalor, ignorance, want'. We can argue that the individualistic emphasis in our country produced many of these social problems, and the case study makes reference to this 'selfish' society. The existence of 'individual families' is not necessarily good for the fabric of our society. This reveals the importance of ensuring that interactionism is combined with other sociological perspectives that also attribute weight to the importance of social factors.

INTERACTIONISM AND CHILDREN

Interactionism can help us in our professional duties as social workers when we are working with children. The perspective emphasises the importance of nurturing creativity in individual children, and also helps us to realise that all children are unique. This is a key strand in the Early Years Foundation Stage (EYFS) in England. Respecting the individual rights of children is regarded as being especially important in the UK, and, as such, we can say that interactionism has made an important contribution to our work with children. There are many advantages to treating children as individuals. If we adopt a collective approach in our work with children, we may appear to be impersonal and lacking an ability 'to make a connection'. It is important that we meet the needs of individual children as far as possible, and a useful way of structuring our professional practice with children is to ensure that we meet their physical, intellectual, emotional and social needs. 'Better practice' can be achieved by meeting these needs in individual children.

There are examples of past social systems that have adopted a collective approach to the detriment of their citizens. The collectivism of the Soviet Union was parodied in novels such as George Orwell's *Animal Farm* and *Nineteen Eighty-Four*. The allegation is made that the egalitarian societies that were claimed to exist were fundamentally corrupt. As opposed to being ideal egalitarian nations, the communist states that existed in the twentieth century and beyond were critiqued as being 'totalitarian' in that the rights of individuals were not respected. An advantage of interactionism appears to be a celebration of individualism. The collective social world is not given priority at the expense of the individual, and the unique nature of each individual is acknowledged and reinforced in inclusive practice. We can argue that many aspects of good practice in the UK emerge from this celebration of individualism. The diversity that characterises our society is based on principles of individualism, and this represents a key contribution made by interactionism to our work with children and families. It reveals how interactionism can help us to improve our practice as social workers.

CASE STUDY

Andrew has moderate learning disabilities, and has a 'key worker' assigned to him in his residential home. Andrew has always struggled with maths, but this began to improve when he worked alongside a specialist maths teacher, who used an individualised learning plan with him. The maths teacher employed a particularly successful learning intervention that was based on using wooden building blocks. Andrew appeared to make an emotional connection with his new maths teacher, and the combination of a specialist intervention alongside this emotional connection appeared to be the reason for his improvement.

REFLECTIVE ACTIVITY 3.4

What is of interest to interactionism and social work about this case study?

In this example, we see how personal learning makes a difference to Andrew. The combination of a teacher who makes a connection with Andrew and a specialist learning plan results in Andrew improving in maths. Interactionist sociologists emphasise the importance of individual characteristics. This reveals the importance of ensuring that we do not treat everyone the same, and is a better way for us to meet individual needs. This can never happen realistically as individuals differ in complex ways. The case study highlights the need to ensure that others are treated according to their individual characteristics. This can enable good practice in our work as social workers. The combination of meeting individual needs and being innovative in our ways of working can result in best practice. In education, we see examples where this results in differentiation of learning, meaning that the different needs of individuals are met through tailored learning activities. As in the case of Andrew, individual needs are met in ways that produce best professional practice. Interactionism is, therefore, a sociological perspective that welcomes creativity and enterprise. This concept of enterprise is interesting for us to consider as social workers. We are not associating being 'entrepreneurial' with enterprise in this example: enterprise is about getting others to think about the world in new and different ways. In the UK, so much education in schools appears to be focused on achieving results. Urban (2009) refers to this as an emphasis being placed on reaching the end destination. In primary, secondary and further education, in particular, we see an increasing focus on obtaining academic results. This can negate a sense of enterprise, where the emphasis on 'thinking outside the box' is lost, with a constant focus being placed on obtaining results. This is the opposite to the interactionist focus on enabling diversity and creativity of thought. In this instance, the advantage of interactionism rests in the generation of creativity and individual best practice. This celebration of diversity and individualism can be traced back to interactionism.

INTERACTIONISM AND MENTAL HEALTH

Mental health is interpreted by interactionists in particular ways, and their sociological theory is able to help us in our professional work as social workers. Interactionists explore how individuals generate meaning in their lives. Interactionist sociologists are interested in the individual interpretation of health and well-being: as opposed to treating categories of the mentally ill in a uniform way, interactionists are more interested in personal interpretations of mental illness. The reflections of authors, including Ken Kesey and Sylvia Plath, are of interest to interactionists. Both of these authors write about their personal experiences of mental illness. As opposed to accepting a 'reality' of mental illness, the two writers focus on the subjective nature of mental illness. The key theme in the work of both of these authors is the personal struggles that are faced by those who have mental health issues. This is a main characteristic of interactionism. The individual experience of mental illness resonates with the interests of interactionists, and this emphasis on individuals and their experiences is particularly useful for social workers. In the UK and elsewhere, there are many challenges with mental illness. We do have a 'national health service' but, regardless of this established health system, there are challenges in treating mental illnesses effectively. This suggests that mental illnesses are complex and that if we wish to understand their complexity, it is important to gather individual experiences of mental illness. The advantage that interactionism provides in this instance is that it enables us to question medical interventions. The Western medical model is not perceived to be necessarily correct in its interpretation of mental illness, and it is therefore important to consider individual experiences. Interactionism provides us with a justification for exploring the individual experiences of those with mental health needs. As opposed to looking at the wider picture, interactionists study particular, idiosyncratic aspects of societies. This focus on the individual experiences of those with mental health needs enables us to explore the complex nature of mental illness. In this way, interactionism can enrich our practice as social workers when we are working with those who have complex mental health needs.

CASE STUDY

Dianne began to experience extreme episodes of anxiety when she was aged 45 years. The anxiety was so extreme that she was unable to leave the house. Dianne was also convinced that other people were constantly watching her and checking on her movements. She went to see a doctor and it was then recommended that she needed to have a separate consultation with a psychologist. Once Dianne's symptoms were investigated further, she was diagnosed with paranoia. She was placed on a series of drugs intended to help her anxiety, however the drug interventions were not effective. If anything, Dianne became even more anxious as a result of this medication.

REFLECTIVE ACTIVITY 3.5

What is of interest to interactionism and social work about this case study?

The case study reveals some of the challenges that exist with medical interpretations of mental illnesses. There is an assumed condition and everyone who is affected by the condition is considered to have the same symptoms. This represents a uniform, 'blanket' approach. In the case study, Dianne's individual needs do not appear to be taken into consideration, and a more effective way of treating Dianne would be to understand the exact nature of her medical condition. Dianne is not necessarily part of a broad category of illness, and it may be that she is just a needy individual who has particular needs like anyone else. It is not necessarily the case that she is 'paranoid'. The medication that Dianne is prescribed appears to exacerbate the problem, causing her to be even more anxious – this occurs because she is placed within a category of mental illness. It is assumed that Dianne, like other 'paranoid' individuals, shares the same symptoms. If we apply interactionism to the case study, we could recommend that her needs should be assessed individually. Dianne is a unique person – there is nobody like her! This is the focus of the interactionists. In view of Dianne's unique characteristics, we need to change our approach to working with her. As opposed to assuming that Dianne is 'paranoid', we should work closely with her in order to identify her particular needs. This is the essence of the Rogerian approach. Rogers argues that it is important to ensure that we resolve 'would/should' dilemmas. This phrase refers to the tension that can exist in our lives over what we 'would' like to happen and what 'should' happen. In this approach, we are encouraged to work with individuals so that their particular needs are met. The advantage of this approach to working with those with mental health needs rests in the recommendation that we should get to know individuals, as it is not appropriate to categorise groups if we are to meet their needs effectively. We can become more aware of this way of working through studying interactionism, which will help enrich our professional practice and enable us to become more effective in working with others.

INTERACTIONISM AND OLDER PEOPLE

Interactionism is helpful for our professional practice as we work with older people. We have noted that older people may experience prejudice and discrimination because they are categorised in stereotypical ways. It may be assumed that all older people show particular characteristics, leading to a whole section of the population being characterised in a particular way. Interactionists emphasise that each person is unique, and this is helpful in enabling best practice in our work with older people. As opposed to viewing older people as sharing characteristics, our professional practice is enhanced by drawing attention to the unique nature of older people. This form of professional practice can help us as we are establishing our professional identity. To get to know those we work with in social work, it is important to spend as much time with them as possible. This allows us to become familiar with particular individuals as we are placed in a position to understand their complex needs. Part of our role as social workers is to ensure as much as possible that we meet physical, intellectual, emotional and social needs. On adopting an interactionist approach, we are more likely to meet these needs. Different older people will have different social needs, and it is not the case that all older people like 'being quiet'. In adopting an interactionist approach, we are more likely to meet these differing social needs. Although older people may have shared physical needs, it is not the case that all older people have the same physical needs. Older people also have different intellectual needs. There may be an assumption that all older people are not as intellectually capable as they were when they were younger, however experience can enrich intellectual ability and it is important to ensure that we work with older people according to their intellectual needs. There may be some older people who are lonely and experience social isolation, but this does not apply to every older person. There are some older people who are socially dynamic. The advantage of interactionism rests in its emphasis on individual characteristics. This can help our professional practice as social workers.

CASE STUDY

Terry is 75 years old. He is very well physically and mentally. He flies to the UK from Canada regularly. Terry does not seem to suffer adversely from 'jet lag'. He walks very well and he enjoys his visits to the UK more than he did when he was younger. Terry claims that his body has adapted to travelling long distances and that it seems easier for him to travel from Canada to the UK now that he is aged 75 years.

REFLECTIVE ACTIVITY 3.6

What is of interest to interactionism and social work about this case study?

The case study reveals that it is not right to assume that all older people are likely to behave in uniform ways. We may assume that older people will not be keen to travel extensively because they are physically and mentally frail, however, in this case study, we see that this is not so with Terry. In spite of his age, Terry travels extensively. Interactionism is useful because the perspective outlines the unique nature of individuals, whether they are old or young. Interactionist sociologists draw attention to the diversity that exists in the world, and the ideas within interactionism help us to celebrate the diversity of human beings. The construction of perception is emphasised by interactionist sociologists, and this allows us to celebrate the exceptions to any given rule. We sometimes see examples of broad, sweeping policies, where individuals can be categorised in particular ways. The advantage of interactionism rests with its emphasis on customising the world we inhabit. As opposed to focusing on what is 'general', an emphasis is placed on what is 'particular'. The diversity that is experienced within children is just as likely to be experienced in older people. If anything, older people are likely to demonstrate more unique characteristics because of their diverse range of experiences, and therefore older people should not be treated in universal ways. The advantage of interactionism is that it draws attention to what is unique and particular. As such, our professional practice as social workers is likely to be enhanced.

INTERACTIONISM AND LEARNING DISABILITIES

Much of the good practice that is evident in the UK today in work with individuals with learning disabilities can be traced back to interactionism. The notion of 'client-centred therapy' is based on the important principle of ensuring that the rights of individuals are respected, and that it is not appropriate to treat all individuals in the same way. A 'condition', whether this is a state of mind or an aspect of physique, should not be used to determine responses to individuals. The excellent practice that is evident in the UK today can be traced back to this important principle. Past practice has categorised groups of individuals negatively, and there has been an assumption that all individuals with 'condition x' are likely to respond in particular ways. This approach can result in examples of negative practice. We have commented on the unfortunate legacy of the asylum in the UK, which is an example of treating others in ways that are 'collective' where similar treatments were issued to individuals in spite of their differences. Variety and diversity were not apparent within professional practice. Individuals with learning disabilities may have characteristics that are shared but it is also important to be aware of their diversity, and the interactionist emphasis that is placed on individualism is more likely to encourage such diversity. Another important development in professional practice that links to interactionism and working with people with learning disabilities is the increasing importance of inclusive education. As opposed to separating learners with learning disabilities and placing them in separate schools, students with learning disabilities are integrated into mainstream education as much as possible. This can produce positive benefits for pedagogy. The alternative practice of removing learners from mainstream education can lead to a segregated and divided education system: just because a learner has a learning disability, does not necessarily mean that they are unable to make a positive contribution in mainstream education. The acceptance of this idea is based on interactionism and the view that individuals are important, a principle which has led to the implementation of the widening participation agenda in the UK. As opposed to excluding learners, as many learners as possible are included within the formal education system. This can result in positive and innovative examples of pedagogy, where the curriculum can be adapted for the needs of learners who can have complex needs. We have witnessed the emergence of 'diversity' in learning as the curriculum is tailored to the needs of individual learners. This can enable a differentiation of learning experience, where learners are encouraged and supported to learn in ways that are innovative and imaginative. This good practice in pedagogy is traced back to interactionism and is another example of how this sociological model can help our professional work as social workers.

CASE STUDY

Simon has learning disabilities and mental health problems. He has a number of professionals working with him. Some of the staff working with Simon can at times treat him in ways that are stereotypical. There is evidence of an assumption that Simon is not able to do what others of his age are capable of doing. Of course, Simon does have learning disabilities, but there are still many things that he is able to do. It is also evident that if it is assumed that Simon cannot do something, he regresses into behaviour that is dependent. This is a further challenge for the staff who are working with him. The more he is treated as if he is unable to do something, the more Simon appears to 'retreat into his own world'.

REFLECTIVE ACTIVITY 3.7

What would interest interactionists about this case study?

Interactionists emphasise the importance of the individual. In the case study, we witness the consequences of assuming that an individual with learning disabilities is not capable of doing what others are able to do. Simon appears to regress in his behaviour once he is treated as someone with learning disabilities. This reveals that if we do not acknowledge the individual ability of others, their life chances diminish. In past generations, there have been countless individuals who have not realised their opportunities or fulfilled their abilities. It has been assumed that they were not capable of achieving something because of 'who they were'. The practitioners who are not demonstrating the best practice are guilty of a similar professional error. They are making a mistake and assuming that he is not capable of doing what others can do. In the case of Simon, we witness an unfortunate 'self-fulfilling prophecy'. It is assumed that he is not able to do something and the consequences are that he becomes less capable. There are examples where those who have belief shown in them go on to do more and more impressive work. With Simon, the opposite is happening. The lack of individualism that is being shown to Simon would be of interest to interactionists.

THE CONTRIBUTION THAT INTERACTIONISM MAKES TO THE RESEARCH PROCESS AND SOCIAL WORK

Interactionism can be traced back to the philosophy of Kant (Audi 1999). The key principle in Kant's work is based on what Audi (1995) refers to as a Copernican revolution of thought. Just as Copernicus discovered that the world revolves around the sun (and not the other way round), so Kant draws attention to the importance of individuals and their understanding of the social world (as opposed to emphasising the importance of forces beyond the individual). When this train of thought is applied to the research process, we experience the power of interactionism, and the result is an exploration of the importance of phenomena. 'Phenomenology' is part of the interactionist legacy and this social theory is closely linked to interactionism. The exploration of individual interpretations of the social world can result in some exciting studies that link to social work practice. This final section of the chapter explores how phenomenology can help us in our work with key client groups in social work. Phenomenology is at the heart of many qualitative research approaches – as opposed to gathering numerical interpretations of the world, qualitative researchers explore individuals and their interpretations of the world. These views, opinions and the beliefs of others are vitally important in our exploration of the social world.

Phenomenology and children

If we are to apply a phenomenological research process to researching an aspect of childhood, we need to go through a number of stages. We need to justify our research ontology – in other words, we need to explain why we are doing our research in this way. We need to clearly identify that we are exploring the views, opinions and attitudes of others within our research process. This will form the basis of the epistemology of our research. In this way, we are contributing new knowledge to the academic community and this can help us in our professional practice as social workers.

An example research question that is based on this approach to research is: 'An exploration of how children in early years are perceived by teaching assistants within a statutory setting.' In this research focus, we can understand 'early years' as birth to seven years old. Once we have identified our research question, we need to consider our research aim and objectives.

The aim refers to the overall research focus, whereas the objectives refer to the specific elements of the research process. It is best not to have too many objectives as this can complicate the research process. Two or three research objectives are sufficient for a small-scale qualitative study. We then need to think about the methods that we are going to use to gather our views and opinions about this research area. In a classic phenomenological approach, it is important to ensure that we select research methods that are suitable for what we want to achieve, and not contradictory to our research approach. It will be unusual to see a research method that is more associated with numerical data if we are adopting a phenomenological approach. An obvious way of gathering data for this research approach is through loosely structured interviews with selected practitioners. It is not essential to interview large numbers of practitioners. We could select 20 practitioners and interview them in order to gather their perceptions for this example research process. We also need to think about the way in which we will analyse the research data that will be generated from this research process. A classic way of analysing data is through thematic analysis. During the analysis of the data, we are seeking to ensure that we gather key themes that have emerged from the research process. We might consider applying computer software to the research process. There are specialist computer software packages that can help us to generate key research themes by identifying key phrases that appear within the transcribed text, an example of which is Nvivo 10. It is also important to identify ways of demonstrating good practice through the research process. We need to demonstrate rigour, and this can be done through collecting data in a number of ways. We might have a first data collection process that is based on interviews with our 20 participants. We can then aim to go to a smaller number of participants in order to complete some further interviews so that we can amplify the themes that are emerging through the research process. It is also important to think about the validity, or authenticity, of our research process. We need to demonstrate that we have received ethical clearance for our research. We also have to show that we are supporting sets of data through triangulating our research. In other words, we do not have just one set of data – we have data that has been obtained from a number of sources and we are complementing this data with published accounts of research from secondary sources.

Phenomenology and mental health

There is much research interest in the subject of mental health. The controversial nature of mental illness and its existence or otherwise is one example of the research interest in mental illness. If we apply a phenomenological focus to this research area can we explore the perceptions of mental illness that are held by selected practitioners. In this research focus, we are interested in exploring what these practitioners think mental illness is, and, in particular, if they think that mental illness is the same or different from other forms of illness. Our research focus in this example could be: 'An exploration of selected practitioners' views of mental illness.' We are interested in identifying the perceptions of the practitioners about mental illness. Our research objectives will seek to identify, explore and analyse the perceptions that the practitioners have about mental illness. We can gather our data through a research methodology that is based on interviews. We could select 20 practitioners who are experienced in working with those who are considered to have mental illness, and aim to return to complete follow-up interviews with a number of key participants who are able to give us particularly rich reflections about mental illness. These follow-up interviews could be completed with 5 participants from the initial 20 research participants. These research methods are appropriate to our research focus and they will enable us to achieve our research objectives.

   In order to embellish our research process, we might apply content analysis to our research by analysing key documents that have been written about mental illness. In content analysis, we are looking to ascertain what the key phrases are that are associated with mental illness. This will complement the interview data that we generate from our primary research participants. The advantage of combining this method of data analysis with thematic analysis is that we will generate a rich source of data that reveals the phenomena that are associated with mental illness. During the research process, we might also consider applying crystallisation, where we explore how our own perceptions interface with the research process. We are considering how we are changing as we interact with our research topic. Perhaps we know someone who has experienced a form of mental illness. If this is the case, how is this influencing our research process? The advantage of crystallisation rests in the emphasis that is placed on the ways in which we change as we reflect on the research process. There is more than an end product within a research process – the final report and the ultimate results are just part of the research process. Reflecting on how we have changed as we engage with the research process is a key part of our experience as researchers, and a vital element of the research process that should be included as opposed to being overlooked. The research process may also become associated with topics that are sensitive and have their considerations. Those with mental illnesses can be extremely vulnerable, so it is important to ensure that we become aware of the ethical protocols inherent within this research. We have a duty of obligation to our research subjects and it is important to ensure that we take the ethics of the research process into consideration at all points in the process.

Phenomenology and older people

If we apply a phenomenological research process in researching older people, we can explore how attitudes towards older people have changed in our society. We need to begin by identifying an appropriate research focus. It is important to select words in our research title that indicate that we are adopting a phenomenological approach. 'An exploration of changing attitudes towards older people' is an example of the sort of research focus that we might adopt. As we are exploring attitudes and per-ceptions, this will be reflected in the research methods that we will adopt.

A possible approach could lead to a methodology that is based on exploring the views of our research participants through a series of focus group discussions, the advantage of which rests in the capacity of the group to generate meaningful discussions through discourse. It is the action of discussion that produces percep-tions about old age, and focus group discussions are a key form of generating phenomenological data. It is also interesting that this form of methodology places an emphasis on the conversational processes that are occurring during the research methodology. It is these conversations that are generating new interpretations about the research question. It is important to think about the skills that we possess as researchers ahead of selecting a particular methodological approach. To complete a successful focus group discussion, we need particular skills, in particular the ability to keep the conversation 'flowing' as smoothly as possible. In order to do this effec-tively, we need to facilitate a positive and enabling social context for our research participants. Some researchers can enable such an environment with ease, whereas others struggle to produce such an environment. We need to recognise the skills that we possess as researchers in order to ensure that the research process works as effectively as possible.

We might also consider applying creative visual methods during the research process. With visual methods, there is clear awareness of the creativity of others as they are involved with the research process. Through using visual props (for example, photographs), we are enabling our research participants to generate visual perceptions of the research area. We could suggest that the participants bring pho-tographs along to the focus group and ask them to reflect on their perceptions of older people by using the photographs as a means of generating social interaction. This creative approach to our methodology is not simply something that 'happens'. We deliberately introduce this strategy into the research process so that meaning is generated by the methods that are employed within the research process. During a phenomenological exploration of the views that are held of older people, we are, therefore, involved with considering how the research process is developing our research question at all stages of the research process. In this way, phenomenology is applied as creatively as possible so that our research methods are used to develop the perceptions that are associated with our research focus.

Phenomenology and learning disabilities

Phenomenology is an ideal research perspective to apply to the study of learning disabilities. Over time, there have been differing interpretations of learning disabilities. This indicates that, as circumstances change, so our perceptions of learning disabilities are also shaped and changed. The term 'learning disabilities' is influenced by time and space. It is a term that has emerged in response to changing perceptions of disability.

If we could travel back to the Victorian era in England, we would hear different terms being used to explain learning disabilities. In nineteenth-century England, religious explanations were given for disabilities. A connection between 'disability' and 'divinity' was evident, and disabilities were explained as being evidence of 'divine disapproval'.

It is only through changing socio-economic circumstances that the perceptions of health and well-being also change. These changing patterns of discourse are of interest to philosophers of knowledge. We have already commented on the impact of the French philosopher Foucault in this book. Foucault writes about the changing patterns of conversations that are evident in societies such as England, and his work explores the changing regimes of power that are apparent in societies. In England, power was vested in formal religion: the sacred space of Christian churches represented power in Victorian England, and a transgression against this sacred space was used to account for disability. With the advent of Western medicine, we begin to see a change in the discourse or conversations about disability. As opposed to witnessing a religious interpretation of disability, we begin to see explanations for disability that are based on science and medicine, and this results in a change in the conversations about disability within society. If we apply a phenomenological approach, to researching perceptions of learning disability, we can use this changing discourse about disability as a focus for our research. Our research question is based on 'exploring the perceptions of learning disability that are shared by selected practitioners'. In this research approach, we are interested in gathering people's perceptions of learning disabilities. We can support our research approach through completing content analysis on key documents that are associated with 'learning disabilities'. We can use computer software (for example, NVivo 10) to help in this regard. In our qualitative multimethod inductive research process, we can gather data through interviews and focus groups. We can select our research participants through purposive and dimensional sampling. We can choose to select 20 key participants who have extensive experience of working with people with 'learning disabilities' and we can ensure that the sample includes participants who have worked in a variety of key roles with those who have learning disabilities. If we analyse this data using thematic analysis, we will be able to generate key themes from this research data. In this way, we will generate appropriate knowledge for our research focus that is based on phenomenological principles.

CONCLUSION

This chapter has explored how interactionism can be applied to social work. We have argued that so many social forms are socially constructed by individuals and their perceptions of the social world, and that different societies at different times have different interpretations of the social world. There is not a rigid acceptance of what is right and what is wrong in the social world. Interactionism draws attention to what is socially constructed in societies by individuals, and this helps our work as social workers across a range of social groups. The chapter has outlined the strengths and weaknesses of interactionism. We have argued that it is important that we maintain a sense of reasonable focus. It is, of course, not right to emphasise the importance of individuals, above and beyond the importance of social structures. Individual interpretations are important, but we have argued that these perceptions of the social world exist beyond individuals, too. It is also important that we are able to see the connection between the meaning that is generated by individuals and the work of social workers.

The world that we inhabit has a meaning that is generated by individuals and so much of our world is a social construction. This world that is created by individuals connects to all the work of social workers. It is the individual interpretation of others that makes such a difference to the lives of children, older people, those with mental health needs and those with learning disabilities. If we think about our own experience of the world, our own perceptions are a vital part of everything that has happened to us. We are not just a 'social group' as we possess an individual identity. We are both biological organisms that are independent as well as being members of social groups – it is our individual identity that makes us who we are. This becomes a key part of the cultural group to which we belong and we are not passive recipients of this culture. Our literary, musical and artistic expressions are fundamentally social but they are also enriched through individual interpretations. Interactionists study human interaction and draw attention to the importance of individual experiences in forming the social world.

This contributes to an enhanced awareness of the best practice in social work. The chapter ended by drawing attention to the vital role that interactionism plays in the research process and social work. The phenomenology that we have reflected on in the research case studies is based on interactionism. In exploring potential research with key groups in social work, we are looking at the generation of meaning: this generation of meaning occurs within individuals and it leads to creativity in human beings. We are interested in exploring how the social world is being constructed in creative ways and interactionism makes a major contribution to this.

CHAPTER 4

CONFLICT THEORY AND SOCIAL WORK

CONFLICT THEORY

Conflict theory is influenced by the ideas of Karl Marx. It is a sociological perspective that is similar to functionalism, with its focus on the social system. Conflict theory is different to functionalism due to the importance that is placed on economics. The perspective explores the material circumstances that produce conflict within social systems. Taylor et al. (2004, p15) emphasise the importance of the concept of 'ideology' to conflict theory. Ideology is produced by beliefs and values which are regarded as being based on material circumstances, and is considered to support the values of the rich and powerful sectors of social groups as opposed to the social system's poor and powerless.

Marx is associated with conflict theory and he was especially interested in those aspects of the social system that appear to be contradictory. He also talked about the terms 'infrastructure' and 'superstructure'. Whereas the infrastructure relates to all tangible aspects of the economic system, the superstructure corresponds to systems of belief and the ideas that are generated from these beliefs. According to Marx, the economic infrastructure has a critical influence on the beliefs and ideas of the superstructure. He draws attention to the importance of social classes. The traditional Marxist emphasis is placed on the existence of two main social groups: a ruling class and a subject class. The contradictory circumstances of these two social classes form the basis of conflict within society according to conflict theorists, and Marx argues that there are a series of fundamental contradictions within capitalist societies. This interest in contradictions links Marx's philosophy to the work of Georg W. F. Hegel, and the exemplification of such contradictory relationships can be seen in the traditional working arrangements for factories. In contrast to the workers who are traditionally regarded as being 'on the factory floor', the factory manager is usually based in a private office. Another example of a contradictory relationship occurs with private ownership: a few powerful individuals own companies, whereas the majority of the population own very little in comparison. Marx argues that these contradictions in society are the basis of instability and conflict. This is the rationale behind the prediction that a revolution will occur within capitalist societies that will lead to a redistribution of wealth and the establishment of a communist society. Marxism is a profound and complex social theory. As noted previously, the emphasis on 'conflict' can be traced back to the influence of Hegel's philosophical idea of a 'thesis, antithesis and synthesis' being present within the social world (Audi 1999). It is acknowledged that a social revolution will only occur when the working class become fully aware of the unfair contradictions that exist within the social system. The argument runs that, until this realisation occurs, the social system is likely to survive because of the 'false consciousness' of the working class. It is only when the working class become fully aware of the implications of social contradictions and of the need to replace the existing social order with a communist society that a social revolution will occur.

Marxist theory emphasies the fundamental link between economic forces and social change (McLellan 1986). The key ingredients of Marxist analyses are captured by Zedner's (2004, p80) argument that the essential components are 'power relations, economic struggle and social conflict'. There are refinements to this understanding of the social world and the work of Bourdieu emphasises the importance of forms of capital that are both 'economic' and 'cultural'. These forms of 'capital' generate 'habitus' that can be understood as being shared social characteristics. Bourdieu's (1986, 1993) work can be developed to argue that there is something that is beyond the material world. This world of cultural values establishes 'fields' of shared social characteristics that interface with human beings. The education, health and political 'fields' have shared characteristics that do not have obvious links to economics. The potentially volatile nature of education, with its 'profits' and 'sanctions', is referred to by Bourdieu (1986, p62) and give space as being akin to a 'market'. He argues that the shared understandings of teaching and learning generate the 'habitus' that becomes associated with education. This draws attention to the conflicts that can exist within the concept of 'cultural capital'. A main purpose of the education system is to enable 'cultural reproduction' that is based on 'differing proportions of the various kinds of capital' (Bourdieu 1986, p62). Bourdieu enriches conflict theory by arguing that the contradictions existing within capitalist societies hold the potential to produce competing ideologies that are characterised by having different understandings of the purpose of human life (Ingleby 2013).

REFLECTIVE ACTIVITY 4.1

Conflict theory refers to the work of Marx to predict that there will be a violent revolution in capitalist social systems. Why do you think that this has only happened in a few societies?

FEEDBACK ON REFLECTIVE ACTIVITY

Part of the difficulty with the work of Marx is that there is a deterministic interpretation of the economy, and this can result in the neglect of the creativity of individuals. With human beings, there are always exceptions to the rule: there are individuals who are creative and this can result in a new arrangement of social conventions; there are inventive individuals who are able to make changes to the social world that are so profound that economic circumstances are transcended. The power of individual charisma can result in economic circumstances becoming less significant. There are a number of individuals in history who have influenced the world in profound ways that are not necessarily based on material circumstances. Some of the great figures of literature have influenced our world through words and the use of language and their material circumstances are unimportant in this context. The power of art and music in human societies does not have an economic basis. Orwell questions the validity of communism and Marxism in his novel *Animal Farm*. The 'will to power' and the ability to realise this 'will to power' becomes more important than economic circumstances in this instance. The creativity of human beings appears to work against the determinism that is located within classical Marxism, so we must be cautious about accepting this philosophy.

CASE STUDY

Ahmed is six years old and he lives in an urban area that has experienced years of neglect. His mother is unemployed and the family's only form of income is from their social security benefits. His father is not part of the family. Although Ahmed is an only child, his mother finds it very difficult to manage financially. Attending school is especially challenging because Ahmed is aware that there are other children in school who have more material possessions than him. He is malnourished and often does not have breakfast, which has resulted in him having difficulties concentrating in school. Although Ahmed has a meal with his mother when he gets in from school, the quality of the food is not as good as it could be due to the family's low level of income. Ahmed also feels the cold and his mother has not always been able to afford a good quality warm winter coat for him. These material circumstances have resulted in him being unable to reach his real educational potential. Although Ahmed's family appear to be 'natural readers', his access to books is limited compared to some of the other children in his class, and this appears to be influencing his self-esteem. He notices what the other children have and he listens to them talking about what they do when they are not in school. Ahmed has been made to feel that he is different. He listens to the other children talking about going on holiday but he has never been on a family holiday. His mother does take him to the local park in the summer holidays but Ahmed wishes he could do something else. The world that he sees on the television appears to be very different to the reality of the life he leads with his unemployed mother.

REFLECTIVE ACTIVITY 4.2

How can conflict theory be applied to this case study?

FEEDBACK ON REFLECTIVE ACTIVITY

It can be argued that many of the difficulties that Ahmed is experiencing could be resolved if his material circumstances were changed. He is described as being 'mal-nourished' and his poor diet will have an inevitable impact on his development. Although Ahmed may be a 'bright' child with academic potential, his material circum-stances may result in feelings of 'low self-esteem'. This is not to say that 'materialism' is a solution to social problems. For Ahmed, child development appears to be influ-enced in profound ways by the distribution of a country's wealth. In a situation of 'haves' and 'have nots', a redistribution of wealth can mean that child development improves and a more equalitarian society is thus produced.

CONFLICT THEORY AND SOCIAL WORK

In contrast to perspectives such as interactionism, conflict theory places an emphasis on the importance of economics. In some ways, the perspective can be seen as being similar to functionalism. As with functionalism, there is a focus on macro socio-logical structures and much attention is given to the ways in which individuals are shaped by social forces that are based on economics, and beyond them as individu-als. This sociological perspective is important for social workers because it reinforces the importance of realising that material circumstances are vitally important in influencing the life chances of those we work with. Conflict theory reinforces the importance of ensuring that the material circumstances of vulnerable groups in society become as robust as possible. The '5 giant evils' that Beveridge drew atten-tion to ahead of the inception of the welfare state (disease, idleness, squalor, ignorance, want) are considered to be contributing factors that shape life chances. The advantage of conflict theory for our professional practice as social workers rests in drawing attention to the importance of material circumstances in social interac-tion. If the material circumstances of others are not met, this will result in conflict within the wider society. The contradictions within societies are regarded as being consequences of the disparity of material circumstances that exists in capitalist soci-eties. It is recommended that there should be a redistribution of wealth so that we see the production of an egalitarian society. This perspective has an obvious appeal to us as social workers. We usually work with vulnerable individuals in society and part of our professional work as social workers requires us to ensure that the material needs of those we work with are addressed. Unless the material basics of others are met, it is impossible to move on to other important elements of professional practice. In becoming aware of the importance of material circumstances, we can become better professionals. In working against the contradictions that are present in societies, we are, in turn, more able to meet the needs of the children and families that we are working with.

CASE STUDY

Kim came from Scotland to London to work as a social worker. She was used to the poverty in Glasgow, but, even so, she was surprised to see how much poverty existed in the East End of London. Kim began working with vulnerable families in Woolwich. On one occasion, in the morning rush hour, she noticed that a man who looked as if he was homeless was lying unconscious at the side of a busy street. Kim was staggered to see how many people walked past this man without stopping to see whether he was alright. The man's head was bleeding. Kim came from a Catholic family in Glasgow, and the sight reminded her of the Bible reading of the good Samaritan. Kim was the only person to stop and ask the man if he needed help.

REFLECTIVE ACTIVITY 4.3

How can conflict theory be applied to this case study?

FEEDBACK ON REFLECTIVE ACTIVITY

The world that is being experienced by Kim in the above case study appears to be a world of contradictions. The commuters are passing on their way to work and they are part of the hustle and bustle of a fast city life. In contrast, someone is lying in the gutter. This reveals the contradictions that are present within a capitalist society. Conflict theorists would be interested in the contradictions that are evident within this case study. These contradictions are regarded as being the product of a capitalist system that is characterised by a few people owning the majority of the means of production.

APPRAISING CONFLICT THEORY

It is also possible to critique conflict theory as with the other sociological perspectives explored in this book. Conflict theory can be perceived as being 'one-dimensional' as too much emphasis is placed on economic forces. Traditional Marxist theorists appear to reduce their explanation of social phenomena to variables that are economic. Lopez and Scott (2000, p80) apply the work of Habermas as an antidote to this tendency to focus on 'the social system' or 'the actions of individuals' or 'the economy'. Habermas (1981) argues that the social structures of capitalist societies are influenced by what is referred to as 'communicative action' and 'purposive action'. According to Habermas (ibid.), 'communicative action' is evidenced through obtaining 'mutual understanding' between those who are operating within a social system. In contrast, 'purposive action' is directed towards achieving goals by 'independent', 'strategic and calculative ways'. Habermas suggests that the shared social meanings of social systems exist alongside the creative interpretations of individuals who may manipulate the social system in order to realise particular goals. It can be argued that this synthesis of functionalist, interactionist and conflict theorist thought provides a potential means of resolving the 'either/or' debate that exists within functionalism, interactionism and conflict theory.

CASE STUDY

Samantha is a children's social worker. She has noticed that a number of the children she works with who come from families living in poverty have poor school attendance. In order to understand why this is happening, Samantha arranges to talk to some of the staff who are based in a local 'Save the Children' office near to where she works. She is made aware that the local schools are suffering from budget cuts and this has resulted in these schools asking parents to make financial contributions to the everyday work of the schools. Talking with the staff lead makes Samantha realise that going to school is challenging for poor children. There are so many indirect costs, including ingredients for cookery lessons and money for school outings. The money that is needed for school uniforms is another example of a cost that appears to have a negative impact on school attendance.

REFLECTIVE ACTIVITY 4.4

What is of interest to social work and conflict theory about this case study?

FEEDBACK ON REFLECTIVE ACTIVITY

The case study reveals the pressures that exist on children and families that come down to financial costs. In our society, we do not have to pay for state schooling, but there are still significant costs for children and families. Conflict theorists are correct to draw attention to the consequences of these costs for children's education. In 1997, Tony Blair's New Labour government were elected to power in the UK and their election mantra was 'Education, Education, Education'. It is interesting to reflect on the material factors that influence children's education. In the case study, the material pressures on poor families are limiting the opportunities for the children to be educated. In England, concern is expressed at the amount of debt that students get into as they borrow money in order to pay for their university tuition fees. This material aspect of education is of interest to conflict theorists, as is the contradictory aspect of the situation: in reality, it is actually the government who are paying for higher education in England. The students have to pay this money back over time. In other words, the actual costs are being met by the government and yet the contradictory claim is made that the costs of university education cannot be met by the state. This contradiction is of interest to conflict theorists.

CONFLICT THEORY AND CHILDREN

Conflict theory is useful to us in our professional work as social workers when we are working with children. The perspective emphasises the importance of becoming aware of how material circumstances influence children and families. Conflict theory also helps us to realise that a change in children's material circumstances has a critical impact on the lives of children and families. This has been a key element in social policy in the UK since the beginning of the twentieth century. Successive governments in England have been made to realise that changing material circumstances are particularly important in influencing the lives of children and families. In this country, a key realisation of the importance of material circumstances for children and families came during the Boer War at the beginning of the twentieth century. For the first time, we saw conscription into the army (Ingleby 2013). During the process of conscription to the armed forces, a significant number of army recruits were identified as being unfit for military duty. This revealed the importance of ensuring that the nation's physical, intellectual, emotional and social needs were being met effectively. The Beveridge recommendations in England in the 1940s were also based on a realisation that it was important to ensure that the material circumstances of children and families were as robust as possible. These recommendations led to the introduction of a welfare state in the UK and the aim of this welfare state was to ensure that the material needs of children and families were met. This reveals that conflict theory has had a powerful influence on policymakers in the UK. A fear of 'socialism' and 'communism' has resulted in our governments attempting to ensure that the material needs of the population are being met. It is the consequences of what might happen if these needs are not being met that appears to form the basis of this 'political fear'. Bismarck realised this in Germany in the nineteenth century (Ingleby 2013). The fear that the needs of the population were not being met and that this would see a rise in support for socialism and communism rests behind the increased investment by the state in services that are designed to help children and families, thereby improving their physical, intellectual, emotional and social development.

CASE STUDY

Leah has moderate learning disabilities. Leah has a 'key worker' and she lives in a residential home. Although Leah is living in a residential home that is supported by social services, her family live in a wealthy suburb of West London. Leah's family have been able to look after her material needs. Her room is nicely decorated, and she is taken on expensive holidays. As she is well looked after materially, her quality of life appears to be good. Despite Leah's learning disabilities, she appears to be content and she also seems to enjoy a good quality of life.

REFLECTIVE ACTIVITY 4.5

What is of interest to conflict theory and social work about this case study?

FEEDBACK ON REFLECTIVE ACTIVITY

In the above case study, Leah's material circumstances appear to make a significant difference to her life as they result in Leah enjoying the life she is leading. This quality of life does not appear to be affected adversely by her learning disabilities. Conflict theorists are interested in experiences that are the opposite of those that Leah is enjoying. There are other children with learning disabilities who live in material circumstances that do not support their physical, intellectual, emotional and social development.

In the following example, the experiences of these children are far from positive. In certain parts of the developing world, the circumstances of children and families are so challenging that they can experience a daily battle for survival, and this results in a desperate situation for these children as their needs are not being met. The natural disasters that occur can draw attention to these challenging circumstances. If a country does not have a robust economic infrastructure, we can witness vulnerable children dying on a vast scale. The children with learning disabilities will not see their needs being met and their experiences will be very different to Leah's. Conflict theorists are interested in these material circumstances and it is important to realise that children's growth and development is influenced in a profound way by the nature of their material circumstances.

In our wealthy Western world, we may associate childhood with images that are predominantly positive. We have so many material possessions in our society that complex games and play are readily apparent. As well as 'free play', we have 'heuristic play', a form of play that results in activities that are 'thought-out' and considered in depth and detail. Play and games are linked to material circumstances. 'Inventive play' may result from a deprivation of material resources. Likewise, complex technological play is linked crucially to material circumstances. The impact of material circumstances on forms of play is of interest to conflict theorists.

CONFLICT THEORY AND MENTAL HEALTH

Mental health is interpreted by conflict theorists by exploring the material circumstances that influence particular mental health needs. This sociological theory is able to help us in our professional work as social workers. Conflict theorists explore the relationships that exist between mental health and material circumstances. They are interested in how mental health links to economic circumstances and, rather than accepting the existence of mental illness, the relationship between mental health and economics is studied. It is clear that mental health is influenced by material circumstances. In the earlier case study in this chapter, the man who was portrayed lying 'bleeding in the gutter' might have been in that situation because he was homeless. In this example, homelessness may exacerbate particular mental illnesses – if you do not have enough money to live on and you are 'on the streets', then this is likely to place strains on both your mental and physical health, so there is a connection between material circumstances and mental health. Conflict theorists are interested in studying this relationship. It can be argued that there are other 'mild' mental illnesses that may be a product of particular levels of income. The upper and middle classes have more disposable income, and this situation might, in fact, exacerbate particular mental illnesses. The disposable income that is available to the individuals in these social classes enables them to have private consultations with specialist medical staff. By talking about your state of mind with these professionals and paying for their services, there is a likelihood that a particular set of conditions may be diagnosed. Conflict theorists are interested in the material power of these groups of people in societies as this material power can influence mental health problems and their diagnosis. This situation is exacerbated by the difficulties that exist when we try to define mental illness. The imprecise nature of mental illness can lead to variability of interpretation. If a person is wealthy enough to pay a physician enough money for enough time to have enough consultations, there is a strong possibility that mental illnesses will be diagnosed. In this way, conflict theory can enrich our practice as social workers when we are working with those who have complex mental health needs.

CASE STUDY

Dwight began to experience 'personality disorders' at the age of 25. He began to hear voices in his head when he was forced to live on the streets in London. Dwight's family background is Afro-Caribbean and he has a history of schizophrenia in his family. It was, however, his material circumstances – living on the streets as a homeless man – that appeared to be the catalyst that led to the emergence of Dwight's schizophrenia.

REFLECTIVE ACTIVITY 4.6

What is of interest to conflict theory and social work about this case study?

FEEDBACK ON REFLECTIVE ACTIVITY

The case study reveals that there is a connection between mental illnesses and material circumstances. This will interest conflict theorists. As mentioned in the case study, the material circumstances that are experienced by Dwight as he lives on the streets appear to be the catalyst for his schizophrenia, as prior to living on the streets, Dwight did not have the symptoms of schizophrenia. It is, however, important to realise that conflict theorists do not have a monopoly on plausible explanations for mental illnesses. There may be a genetic explanation for some mental illnesses, as discussed later in this book. The genetic theory behind schizophrenia identifies the link between family members with schizophrenia and the development of this condition in their offspring. In this example, the key cause for Dwight's schizophrenia might be his inherited condition, therefore the genetic reasons for schizophrenia need to be taken into consideration in this example.

We have seen that difficulties can arise if we limit explanations for mental illnesses to just one of the sociological perspectives. In fact, an explanation that combines sociological perspectives may be a more effective way of explaining particular medical conditions.

By adopting this holistic approach, a more effective explanation for Dwight's situation can be attained. His genetic background combines with his personal circumstances and this gives us a powerful explanation of why he is experiencing symptoms of mental illness. The advantage of combining sociological perspectives in this example ensures that we do not become reductionist in our explanation of complicated social circumstances. There is no single way of explaining the social world. By combining perspectives, we achieve a more informed explanation for what is happening. We avoid making a generalisation that explains the social world in one way. This combination of perspectives (or holism) enables us to have a more effective platform on which we can base our professional practice.

CONFLICT THEORY AND OLDER PEOPLE

Conflict theory is helpful for our professional practice as we work with older people. We have noted that older people may experience challenging social circumstances compared to other sectors of the population, and conflict theorists draw attention to the material circumstances that allow this discrimination to occur. We have seen already that older people can be physically vulnerable, leading them to be placed in 'at risk' categories. The assumption of a physical state that is 'not robust' is a common view of old age in our society. Conversely, in 'non-traditional' contexts, older people may be valued because they are perceived as being 'wise' and 'experienced'. Conflict theorists are interested in how and when this understanding of older people is applied. It is argued in this book that the perception of older people is not very positive in our society, and this is possibly due to material circumstances. This will be of interest to conflict theorists. In the UK, it is predicted that there will be more people aged over 65 years than those who are aged under 16 by the year 2020. If this occurs, we will have a 'top-heavy' society. There is a potential situation of more people being supported in society and fewer people generating wealth for the economy, and this set of material circumstances will present challenges for our society. The material reality of this demographic situation is a possible explanation for the perception of older people in developed societies. They may be perceived to be a 'drain on resources' and this is a material perception of older people. The comparative 'rarity' of older people in developing societies may explain why they tend to be accepted in ways that are at times reverential. The worship of older people and ancestors that can occur in traditional cultural contexts may be a consequence of a social situation that is the opposite to that happening in the West. In our society, the Beveridge reforms that resulted in the welfare state have supported the improvement of material circumstances for older people. The perception of older people is influenced by material factors. The importance of ensuring that older people are looked after has become a key part of social policy. In the UK today, a number of older people appear to be financially better off than those who are working. In this example, perhaps a 'New Jerusalem' has been created for older people as their material needs are being met.

CASE STUDY

Margaret is 81 years old. Although she does not have a private pension, she has a state pension and thinks that she has been well looked after by the state. This pension provides Margaret with enough money to live on each month. Margaret also receives other benefits. When the winter comes, she receives a 'winter fuel allowance'. These supportive material conditions enable Margaret to enjoy a good quality of life.

REFLECTIVE ACTIVITY 4.7

What would interest conflict theorists and social workers about this case study?

FEEDBACK ON REFLECTIVE ACTIVITY

The case study reveals the importance of the material circumstances of older people. If older people have their physical needs met, this is more likely to produce a sense of emotional well-being. In the case study, Margaret has a sense of emotional well-being because her physical needs are being met. The vulnerability that can be experienced in old age may be exacerbated if an individual's material circumstances are precarious. In the UK, there has been discussion of the consequences of a situation of 'precarity', where large numbers of individuals are not having their material needs being met. The occurrence of precarity can lead to mental health problems that begin as mild neuroses and turn into debilitating psychoses. Conflict theorists argue that it is especially important to meet the physical needs of individuals. A state of precarity is never good for the vulnerable sectors of a society and older people may form a significant element of this 'at risk' sector. In the UK, looking after older people has a moral significance. Our sense of 'civilisation' depends upon how we look after our older population, and we would not wish to be recorded as a society that is perceived to be 'nasty, brutish and short' (Hobbes, 1651/ 1962). Ideally, we are characterised as a society that looks after the vulnerable. Conflict theory contributes to this development of a morally strong society by increasing awareness of the importance of the material circumstances of older people. In becoming more aware of these circumstances, our professional practice as social workers is likely to be enhanced.

CONFLICT THEORY AND LEARNING DISABILITIES

Conflict theorists are traditionally associated with vulnerable sectors of society and individuals who are not able to look after themselves because of their material circumstances. We have argued in this chapter that conflict theory can be traced back to the philosophy of Hegel and the conceptualisation of a 'thesis, antithesis and synthesis' (Audi 1999 p315). In this philosophy, societies are not regarded as being 'static' – they are always moving. In this state of flux, followers of this philosophy suggest that inequality should be challenged. This notion of challenging inequality has resulted in the rise of the disability rights movement, whereby the inequality that is experienced by disabled people is now challenged. It can be argued that this is a significant contribution that has come from conflict theory, and that the rise in awareness of the importance of promoting the rights of disabled people equates to the values of conflict theory. It is argued that it is not right to accept that disabled people are 'second class citizens' – action is necessary in order to challenge this situation of inequality. A call to 'action' is a key theme in the work of French philosopher Maurice Blondel (1893).

In our society, disabled people appear to have been inspired by the civil rights movements of other disadvantaged groups in society. Alongside feminism and the civil rights movement, we see a rise in the numbers of disabled people who are campaigning for equality of opportunity. The positive message coming from conflict theory is that it is important to oppose oppressive and unfair relationships. In the field of learning disabilities, there is a powerful movement in our society that represents disabled people and champions their rights. Those with learning disabilities are no longer portrayed as being a sector of society that is different from the rest of society with regards to rights – it is more that the needs of these individuals differ. The message of reacting against oppressive practice in this instance has been very positive for disabled people, and one positive consequence has been a rise in the appreciation of particular categories of disability. This has led to positive and innovative practice in our society, as the social world has been adapted for the needs of disabled people who can have complex needs. We have witnessed the acceptance of 'diversity' in society as our social world has become tailored to the needs of disabled people. The disabled members of society are encouraged and supported so that their needs are met. This good practice in disability can be traced back to conflict theory and it is another example of how this sociological model can help our professional work as social workers.

CASE STUDY

Mark has enrolled on a degree programme at a university that is located within an old medieval town. Most of Mark's lectures are in different locations and it can be a challenge getting into some of the buildings. The university timetable is planned centrally and, in his first week of lectures and seminars, Mark experiences all sorts of difficulties arriving at the teaching sessions on time. He is concerned that this is reinforcing a perception of students who are in wheelchairs being unable to manage the same practical tasks as able-bodied students. Mark joins the university's students' union and he is put in touch with other disabled students who are planning to raise awareness of the difficulties that they are experiencing.

REFLECTIVE ACTIVITY 4.8

What would interest conflict theorists about this case study?

FEEDBACK ON REFLECTIVE ACTIVITY

In this chapter, we have stated that conflict theorists are especially interested in raising awareness of issues associated with social justice. This example highlights an issue of social justice – it does not seem right that Mark is experiencing these difficulties just because he is in a wheelchair. Conflict theory encourages us to protest about injustices like this, and draws attention to the contradictions that are present in societies that are based on capitalist economics. In the above example, there is a contradictory situation: disabled students are provided with an opportunity to go to university, but the design of the university buildings prevents them from accessing this education. Perhaps when Mark meets the other students who are experiencing these challenges he will be able to protest effectively about what has happened to him? The students can raise awareness of the importance of architects working with educators so that the future infrastructure can take the needs of those with disabilities into consideration. Such a development is surely not too much to ask? The use of a protest movement to alter a world that is 'not just' will interest conflict theorists.

CONCLUSION

This chapter has explored how conflict theory can be applied to social work. We have argued that so many social forms are fundamentally influenced by material circumstances, and that every society is influenced to some extent by the economic means of production even though different societies at different times have different interpretations of the social world. Conflict theory draws attention to what is shaped by material circumstances, which is helpful in our work as social workers across a range of social groups. The chapter has outlined the significant contribution that conflict theory makes to our professional work as social workers. Of course, we should not be overly obsessed with the economic means of production, which can be seen as a criticism of conflict theory. Economic forces are important, but we have argued that the world is not entirely determined by the means of production. It is important for us to realise the significance of economic forces and this does help our work as social workers, but there are other variables influencing human societies that are beyond economic forces. Our human world is constructed by individuals who engage with social forms, and our world is created by individuals as opposed to being determined by economic forces. It is this combination of structure and agency that is the basis on which we engage in our work with children, older people, those with mental health needs and those with learning disabilities. We have argued in this book that our own perceptions are a vital part of everything that happens to us. We are not just formed by the means of production as we have an individual identity that is unique – we are biological organisms that are both independent and influenced by the means of production. It is this combination of being an individual and being shaped by economic forces that helps in making us who we are. Material forces are important, but it is equally necessary to realise that we are not passive recipients of material forces. Our literary, musical and artistic expressions are fundamentally influenced by material circumstances but they are also influenced by individual circumstances. The debate over material determinism is a critical part of conflict theory. The classical Marxism that places a key emphasis on economics has been refined by later neo-Marxist theorists. In this chapter, we have cited Bourdieu as an example of an academic who is able to refine the argument that we are determined by economic forces. Bourdieu draws attention to the 'capital' that is associated with 'culture', and this highlights the importance of focusing on culture in its own right. This argument enables us to reflect on aspects of the social world that are beyond economic forces. Bourdieu's work does not rest uneasily with individuals and their creativity. Creativity in human beings is not just a form of 'false consciousness'. The creative aspects of human beings are as crucially involved with shaping the world as are material circumstances. In combining our awareness of the importance of material circumstances and individual creativity, we can apply the importance of conflict theory to our work as social workers.

The complex relationship between material circumstances and individual creativity is revealed in the work of the novelist D.H. Lawrence. In his novels, including *Sons and Lovers*, Lawrence writes about the challenges that were present as he grew up in a mining village in Nottinghamshire, in the nineteenth century. Lawrence's father was a miner and Lawrence was fundamentally influenced by the material circumstances of his life, as the son of a miner. Yet, he was affected by these material circumstances in complex ways: the means of production in Lawrence's life became a catalyst that inspired him to become a writer. He uses the experience of growing up in a mining village to write about the unique nature of mining communities. The world of *Sons and Lovers* is, indeed, a contradiction. The title of the book is ambiguous. Lawrence writes about a world in a way that actually shapes what is happening. As opposed to viewing Lawrence as being shaped by material circumstances, it is more accurate to consider that he is forming our understanding of this world. The pit villages of nineteenth-century Nottinghamshire are no more, but the world that Lawrence has created in his novels is still present. In this instance, individual creativity is outlasting the means of production. This reveals the challenges that are present if we regard the world as being shaped by economic forces. In this chapter, we have seen that economic forces are important. It is, however, essential for us to acknowledge the creative engagement with economic forces that is present within human societies. Lawrence is one example of many of this creativity. These examples reveal the importance of ensuring that we consider individual creativity alongside structural forces. This dilemma is present with other perspectives in sociology. The overemphasis that is placed on social structures that is found in other sociological perspectives (for example, functionalism) is a similar issue. Conflict theorists are correct to draw attention to the importance of the means of production as we are developing our professional practice as social workers, however it is necessary for us to acknowledge the importance of individual creativity as we engage with economic structures.

CHAPTER 5

CHILDREN, SOCIOLOGY AND SOCIAL WORK

INTRODUCTION

This chapter considers the concept of childhood, and what our three key sociological perspectives focus on when they consider childhood. The chapter draws on cross-cultural comparisons of childhood to outline that the concept of childhood is created. Human beings are a product of both biological and social factors. The chapter outlines that in becoming aware of the social creation of 'childhood', social workers can become reflexive (in other words, we think about the reality of child-hood). This allows us to reflect on the concept of childhood and question previously 'fixed' definitions.

FUNCTIONALIST INTEREST IN CHILDHOOD

Functionalists can be regarded as placing an emphasis on 'the wider wood' as opposed to looking at 'the individual trees' making up the wood. Functionalist sociologists such as Durkheim and Parsons are more interested in the conceptualisation of child-hood that exists within a society and the subsequent implications that this has for the social world. If there is no social understanding of childhood within a society or a social group, we only have young and old human beings. Functionalist sociologists are interested in the type of social circumstances that lead to the social creation of the concept of childhood. As UK society modernised, childhood as a social concept became increasingly important. The identity of childhood became defined by particular social conventions, for example children were expected to go to school and not to work. Functionalists are interested in how societies preserve this sense of identity. Just as a body has its main organs, so our societies have their key social institutions. These social institutions are regarded by functionalists as being responsible for preserving and developing this shared understanding of childhood. The legal system in a society will introduce laws to preserve this definition of childhood. For example, there are laws in societies such as the UK that prevent children from being forced to go to work. The health and education systems also preserve and enhance this shared understanding of childhood. In the UK, all children are offered particular inoculations at particular ages to preserve their health and well-being. All children are also expected to go to school at a particular age and remain in school until the age that is preserved in law. Social workers are helped by this social understanding of childhood. Part of the role of a social worker is to protect the rights of children under the law. It is important to realise that these laws about childhood have been generated by the social system – they are more than the views of individuals. As such, these laws deserve to be respected and taken into consideration. The laws surrounding childhood are a representation of conventions about the social world. Functionalist sociologists are also interested in how different societies produce different laws to protect children. Although many societies have laws concerning children, these laws depend on cultural variables: there are no universal laws applying to all societies. Although attempts have been made to protect all children under the law (for example, via the United Nations Convention on the Rights of the Child), variable social arrangements make it challenging to apply this legislation in every instance. This should lead social workers to realise that there is no omnipotence within social law. The protection of children can be subverted just as the laws of the land can be subverted. A peril with the functionalist project may manifest itself within the implication that wider social factors are inherently more important than the work of conscious individuals.

INTERACTIONIST INTEREST IN CHILDHOOD

Interactionists can trace their sociological approach back to the philosophy of Kant. As we have seen, Audi (1999) draws attention to the Copernican revolution of thought that characterises Kant's philosophy. As opposed to asking 'big questions' about childhood, interactionists are more interested in the perceptions of individual children and their families. An interactionist is interested in how the world of the individual child is perceived and constructed. Interactionist sociologists like Weber explore the nature of *verstehen* or 'understanding' that is occurring within the child's mind. The advantage of this approach to sociology rests within the flexible awareness that childhood is a part of the human world that evidences individual understanding. Each child experiences childhood in a unique way. Heraclitus is the Greek philosopher who made famous the idea that nobody steps into the same river twice. This saying reveals the importance of accepting the individual nature of the social world. The interactionist account of the social world enables us to consider why we get such variety within the social world. If each child does have a unique understanding of childhood, we need to consider the importance of individual interpretations of childhood. The benefit of becoming aware of this understanding of the social world is realised on considering that, within any society, there will be unique perceptions of childhood. As opposed to focusing on wider social conventions, interactionists choose to study the personal perception of these social conventions within individual children. Social workers are helped by this understanding of childhood by becoming aware of the individual rights of children. A benefit of interactionism enables us to treat children as unique individuals, the merits of adopting an interactionist approach allow social workers to meet the unique needs of children. In the UK, an emphasis is placed on the importance of each child – children are regarded as being 'original'. As opposed to thinking about collective needs, the advantage of this sociological approach is that each child's individual needs are taken into consideration. Interactionist sociologists are also interested in multiculturalism. Each child is regarded as having the potential to contribute to a rich experience of child-hood in a varied cultural way. This approach to understanding childhood can be criticised because so much emphasis is placed on individual interpretations that we may become unable to make generalisations. There is no social work practice that occurs between a social worker and a child in isolation. There are always broader social factors that also need to be taken into consideration, and there are patterns of behaviour that need to be considered so that we can make generalisations. No person is an island! A difficulty with the interactionist approach can manifest itself within the suggestion that individuals are more important than social structures. As we have seen, the social world is a combination of what is social and what is individual.

CONFLICT THEORY AND CHILDHOOD

Conflict theorists are interested in how economic forces influence social groups. This sociological perspective explores the economic factors influencing the lives of children and families. The sociologists associated with this perspective are particularly inter-ested in the ways that economic factors shape the lives of children. We can see this at first hand in the paintings of Augustus Edwin Mulready which depict the lives of children in Victorian Britain. Many of the paintings reveal the challenging circum-stances experienced by these children due to poverty and the inadequate infrastructure characterising Victorian Britain. Children were often living in impoverished condi-tions and these squalid conditions of the emerging cities resulted in illness and poor health. Children were expected to work for a living. Mulready depicts this in his painting *fatigued minstrels*, where little children are featured playing music on the streets in order to make a living. They have laboured so much that they are exhausted and are lying asleep on the street. In this example, the nature of capitalism witnesses a fundamental consequence for children and families. Marx draws attention to the inequalities existing within capitalist economies, where the means of production are controlled by a minority of the population. Mulready's paintings often depict the lives of the wealthy minority by highlighting their wealth and opulence in contrast to the children who are struggling on the streets. Marx argues that this social world is a consequence of economic forces, and the argument runs that, if we change the nature of the economy, we will change the experiences of children and families. In Britain, the

Labour Party based many of its social reforms on the ideas of conflict theorists. Marx predicted that a violent social revolution would follow if these social circumstances were left unchanged, and the tension resulting from social inequality would generate a state of revolution once the population were mobilised against the owners of the means of production. The reforms in Britain from the Labour Party after 1945 were based on the wish to improve social circumstances. The emergence of the National Health Service, state-built housing, social security benefits, state education and social work resulted from the political attempts being made to eliminate what were referred to as 'social evils'. The advantage of conflict theory rests in the insight that the perspective gives us into how the lives of children and families are affected by economic forces. Change the nature of the economy and the lives of children and families are subsequently improved. Economic factors shape the experiences of children and families and conflict theory draws attention to the importance of economics.

DIFFERENT CHILDREN, DIFFERENT FAMILIES, DIFFERENT CULTURES AND SOCIAL WORK

Haralambos and Holborn (2008) focus on the importance of George Peter Murdock's (1949) contribution to understanding the nature of human children and families. Murdock explores whether or not the family is 'a universal social institution'. He addresses this question by summarising the research that exists on family characteristics in 250 societies. These families are situated in 'hunter-gatherer bands' and 'large-scale industrial societies'. Murdock's key finding is that 'every human society is characterised by the family'. The definition that is used for the family is of 'blood relations living together'. This important research proposes that 'the family' is a 'universal social institution' (Ingleby et al. 2014).

REFLECTIVE ACTIVITY 5.1

If the family is a universal institution, what are the consequences for social workers?

FEEDBACK ON REFLECTIVE ACTIVITY

We have seen that the interactionists emphasise the importance of human beings who create and generate social meaning. This model of sociology draws attention to how creative individuals make the social world. It is, however, important to realise that the human world is not necessarily a 'blank canvas' on which anything can be drawn. There are elements of the human world that are not just social creations. Murdock's (1949) research stands the test of time and is still important today. The common feature across all the diverse social groups within the research is 'the family'. This suggests that the family is an important part of all human societies and, as such, the family needs to be supported by social workers. This vital social organisation is essential to us as human beings. As opposed to working against the principle of the family, social workers need to base their professional practice on wider social realities. The importance of the family needs to be a central principle driving forward social work practice. Of course, not all families are 'functional', and the reason for social work can be based on a realisation that a particular family is not working as it should. It is, however, important to work with that family structure as opposed to working against the principle of the family. Murdock's (1949) research reveals that families are important within societies. Whenever possible, social workers need to ensure that families are supported so that the physical, intellectual, emotional and social needs of children and families are protected.

THE NAYAR FAMILY STRUCTURE AND A DIFFERENT SENSE OF CHILDHOOD

Kathleen Gough's (1959) research on the Nayer, a social group in Kerala in Southern India, can be used to develop the argument that there are different understandings of the family within other cultural groups. These different understandings of the family reveal that there are very different experiences of childhood in different societies. Gough's ethnographic description of the Nayar reveals that girls in Nayar society have arranged marriages before they reach puberty. Once the ritual marriage is completed, a 'husband' does not live with his 'wife'. The social conventions in Nayar society are such that husbands are under no obligation to have any contact with their wives. The only social expectation is that the wife is expected to attend her husband's funeral upon his death.

Once a girl does reach puberty, she is allowed to take what are referred to as 'sandbanham' husbands. These 'visiting men' are portrayed by Gough as being 'professional warriors'. Gough records that a sandbanham husband tended to arrive at the home of one of these available women in the evening, have sexual intercourse with her, and leave before breakfast the next day. In this social group, Gough reveals that Nayar men could have unlimited numbers of sandbanham wives, and women could have up to 12 visiting husbands.

Nayar society reveals a different experience of family life to most other societies. A man and wife do not experience a conventional lifelong union. Moreover, sandbanham husbands are not expected to have obligations towards the children of their wives. Gough (1959) reveals that, although the 'father' of a child was expected to pay a fee of 'cloth and vegetables' to the midwife attending the childbirth, this 'father' was not necessarily the biological father of the child. When a Nayar woman became pregnant, the only expectation was that 'someone' acknowledged that they were the child's father. In this social group, fatherhood is more of a social convention than in some of the other social groups revealed by Murdock's research.

Gough also draws attention to the absence of economic relations between husbands and wives in Nayar society. Although husbands might provide gifts for their wives, there is no expectation that a husband should be an 'economic provider' for his wife. Gough reveals that such a practice was regarded by the Nayar as being socially inappropriate. An economic unit was established by brothers, sisters and sisters' children and daughters' children. The leader of this family was the eldest male. Ingleby et al. (2014) describe Nayar society as an example of a 'matrilineal' family. The family is understood as being based on female biological relatives. Marriage provides no role in establishing households, socialising children or providing economic needs. Sexual relations are socially appropriate between couples who neither live together nor cooperate together economically. Ingleby et al. (ibid.) use this work to reveal that there is no universal interpretation of the family.

REFLECTIVE ACTIVITY 5.2

What are the advantages of the Nayar family?

FEEDBACK ON REFLECTIVE ACTIVITY

The Nayar experience of family life appears to be very different to our experience of nuclear families. There does not appear to be a clear correlation between sex and the family. In our society, art, books and music have examples of a legal father being portrayed as an ideal father. In our culture, a legally sanctioned family may be exemplified by a man and a woman who are married under the law. Of course, times have changed and there are now other types of family in our society. Despite this social change, the media images over the years have been based on an understanding that the nuclear family is the best type of family. In Nayar society, this different type of family may have advantages. There appears to be a loose concept of the family and there are not the same social conventions that equate sexual relations with family identity. This can have its advantages if the children in Nayar society are free from the oppression that can be experienced within some of the families in our society. This 'oppression' is outlined by authors including D.H. Lawrence, who writes powerfully about domestic violence. If domestic violence is avoided through having a loose family structure, this could be perceived as an advantage of the Nayar family structure.

The next section of the chapter develops the theme that childhood experiences differ according to family type. In addition to the presence of 'cultural differences', the concept of 'the family' has changed over time. The experiences of childhood are linked to changing social conventions, as different epochs are characterised by different types of family. The family is not fixed or rigid. In becoming aware of these changing family types, which can vary according to time and place, your social work practice is likely to become enhanced as you can meet complex individual needs.

THE CHANGING FAMILY OVER TIME AND PLACE

As well as differing according to culture, the family also varies through 'time' and this has a significant bearing on the experience of childhood. At different times in history, there have appeared different forms of family. Haralambos and Holborn (2008) develop this concept in drawing attention to the different family types that existed within pre-industrial societies in comparison to industrial societies.

Anthropologists such as I.M. Lewis (1981) reveal that wider kinship relationships are particularly important within pre-industrial societies. It may be difficult to rely on a nuclear family for resources, so wider kin become integral to the operation of the social group. These kinship groups are more established in pre-industrial societies. They are formed over mutual rights and obligations. The importance of wider kin in pre-industrial societies is revealed by Haralambos and Holborn (2008) with the case study of the Pomo First Nation in Northern California in the USA. In this culture, the family are regarded as being 'all important'. There is no sense of a 'state' or a social group beyond the family. As opposed to experiencing childhood within 'nuclear families', many pre-industrial children experienced childhood within what Haralambos and Holborn (2008) refer to as 'classic extended families'. These families are typified by the importance of 'extended families'. Haralambos and Holborn (2008) exemplify the traditional Irish patriarchal farming family that sees property passing down through male relatives as an example of pre-industrial family type. Social and economic roles appear to come together within this form of family. The typical 'extended family' consists of a husband, his wife, their children, his parents and unmarried brothers and sisters. The family are portrayed as working together to become a 'production unit' in order to maintain economic viability.

REFLECTIVE ACTIVITY 5.3

What do you think are the challenges of this form of family in pre-industrial times? In the previous reflective activity, we focused on the advantages of the Nayar family structure. What are the disadvantages of pre-industrial family structures?

FEEDBACK ON REFLECTIVE ACTIVITY

Although it is important to make sure that we do not generalise about one type of family structure, we can see challenges that exist for families in pre-industrial times. The family structure appears to be influenced by the economic reality of the pre-industrial world. The presence of different types of kin within the family appears to be generated out of economic necessity. The wider family is being used in order to provide economic sustenance. This is not ideal: it may be better if the family was determined by choice and obligation as opposed to just a sense of necessity. The wider economic reality influencing family structures in pre-industrial times produces an experience of family life that is rigid. Today, we experience a richness of family life within a consumer society. We can take the basic requirements for life for granted, and this can allow us to have an experience of family life that is diverse. It is important, however, to remember that our experience of family life is not absolutely better now than in pre-industrial times. The family differs and changes according to variable circumstances that are not absolute.

PRE-INDUSTRIAL FAMILIES

Peter Laslett (1972) reveals that 'time' as well as 'space' influences family type. Laslett's work explores how pre-industrial conditions in England influenced the structure of families, and reveals that from 1564 to 1821, only 10 per cent of households included kin who were beyond the nuclear family. Laslett (1972) notes that this percentage was the same for England in 1966, and draws on data from the USA to reveal that pre-industrial societies are not necessarily associated with 'extended families'. This goes against the assumption that the nuclear family is a creation of industrialisation. Ingleby et al. (2014) argue that if this is the case, it might mean that there are more similarities in children's experiences of the family in pre-industrial times than we might automatically assume. In other words, it is not necessarily the case that the experience of family life in pre-industrial times was so different to our experiences of the family today. Laslett (1972) goes on to argue that the nuclear family was the typical family type in northern France, the Netherlands, Belgium, Scandinavia, parts of Italy and in Germany. In contrast, in Eastern Europe, Russia and Japan, the extended family was more common (Laslett 1972). Laslett's work challenges the argument that there is a connection between the nuclear family and the Industrial Revolution. This argument is supported by Berger (1983), who equates the nuclear family with the 'modernity' that is conducive to industrial development. Berger argues that nuclear families encourage individuals to be self-reliant and independent. These qualities are considered to be vital as they enable 'industrial entrepreneurs' to flourish.

Haralambos and Holborn (2008) emphasise the importance of Laslett's (1972) work. The notion of 'tribes' or 'clans' of people existing together in pre-industrial

Britain is not necessarily the case. It is also not the case that industrialisation necessitated the advent of the nuclear family. Laslett's work, however, is not accepted as being the unequivocal truth. Michael Anderson (1980) presents some contradictory evidence in Laslett's research. Anderson argues that, although the average household size may have been fewer than five people, the majority of the population of pre-industrial Britain (53 per cent) lived in households of six or more people. Anderson also reveals that in some cultural contexts, for example Sweden, extended families were very common. This suggests variation of family type across Europe. One example cited by Anderson (1980) reveals that 'gentry' and 'yeoman' farmers tended to have much larger households than the average. This explains why Anderson is critical of the concept of a 'Western nuclear family'. We can use this research as evidence that it is unwise to claim that one type of family is dominant in pre-industrial times. What appears to be more significant is the prevailing sense of expectation within cultural groups. It appears to be the diversity and creativity of human beings alongside their material circumstances that influences how the type of family develops. In becoming aware of different family types and the circumstances influencing family structures, your practice as a social worker can be helped as you are more able to meet the diverse needs of individual family members.

REFLECTIVE ACTIVITY 5.4

Do you think that 'family type' has a significant impact on children's experience of childhood?

FEEDBACK ON REFLECTIVE ACTIVITY

It may be assumed that there is an 'ideal family type', perhaps a mother, father and children, but the evidence from social science suggests that it is not the type of family that is the crucial factor. The structure of the family is of less importance than what is actually happening within the family. As long as the children are loved and cared for, the structure of the family is a less significant factor. If every child lived in a nuclear family, their experiences of childhood would differ despite the same family structure being in place. Material circumstances and the health of the individuals within each family appear to be essential if the experience of family life is to be positive. If a family experiences poverty or if family members have mental illness, this appears to be more significant than the actual structure of the family. Awareness of these socio-economic realities could help to improve your effectiveness as a social worker.

CHANGING TIMES AND CHANGING FAMILIES

This chapter outlines some of the complexity that influences childhood through time and space. Of course, we have family arrangements that outlive our own experiences of family life. Were it possible for people from the Victorian era to see our family lives, perhaps those individuals would be able to identify with current family experiences. We also have an 'ideal family' that may be seen as removed from the reality of our own family life. This is described by Leach (1997) as the 'cereal packet image' of the family. Leach uses this image to describe the 'typical family' that is featured in some UK breakfast cereal advertisements. The 'typical family' is portrayed as 'dad, mum and the children' as if this type of family is somehow ideal. UK society today is characterised by diverse families, a trend that has been emerging over the years.

Rapoport et al. (1982) identify that only 24 per cent of UK families consist of married couples, children and one 'breadwinner'. This indicates that the UK has witnessed a decline in the number of households that are characterised by married couples looking after dependent children. Haralambos and Holborn (2008) reveal that the percentage of UK households with married couples and dependent children declined from 38 per cent in 1961 to 24 per cent in 1992. It is also important to acknowledge the rise of single person households. Haralambos and Holborn (2008) state that this figure rose from 2.5 per cent in 1961 to 10.1 per cent in 1992. In other words, over time, the nature of the family has changed. This changing family structure is also found in other European countries (Rapoport et al., 1982). The percentage of children in the UK living in families with two married parents fell from 72 per cent in 1997 to 63 per cent in 2009 (Office for National Statistics). By 2015, there were 2.8 million single parent households. This form of family type has increased from 1996 to 2015 (ONS) and the findings reveal other key statistics about the nature of family life. Cohabiting families, with parents who are not married, account for 17% of families in the UK. This reveals that children's experience of childhood may be different to previous times when there was social pressure to be 'legally married'.

REFLECTIVE ACTIVITY 5.5

The Office for National Statistics reveal that there are more single parent households in the UK now than ever before. What are the advantages and disadvantages of this family type?

FEEDBACK ON REFLECTIVE ACTIVITY

There is no ideal type of family, or ideal time in history to be part of a family. All forms of family life have consequences that are either positive or negative. There are advantages and disadvantages to being raised in single parent families. If a single parent has a number of children to look after, this can be a challenge as it is difficult to give each child the attention required, and it can also be difficult to provide the material resources that are needed by the family. It could be construed from the above example that it might be better to have parents who can give the children the attention and the material resources that they need to develop effectively, however this depends on circumstances. For instance, if both parents argue frequently, an unpleasant atmosphere may result within the household, and it might therefore be better for the children to live in a single parent household.

SINGLE PARENTS AND SINGLE PARENT HOUSEHOLDS

The previous section reveals that by 2015, there were 2.8 million lone parent families in the UK. The sociological interest in single parent families is extensive. The interest in single parent households goes back a long time. Haralambos and Holborn (2008) explore the the occurences that have led to family separation, and highlighted the connection between rising divorce rates and rising numbers of single parent households. In the UK, from 1971 to 1991, the proportion of single mothers who were divorced rose from 21 per cent to 43 per cent (Ingleby et al. 2014). From 1971 to 1991, the figure changed from 16 per cent to 34 per cent (Ingleby et al. 2014). David Morgan (1986) uses this data to argue that UK society evidences differing expectations of marriage. This appears to be the case with women's expectations of marriage, and the notion that 'married for life' appears to depend more on the perceived quality of the relationship.

In the UK, this trend appears to have been developing for many years. It is a trend commented on by Haralambos and Holborn (2008), with the argument that single parenthood is not 'frowned upon' as it used to be. In other words, the stigma attached to single parenthood appears to have diminished. The phrases that were applied to children who are born to single parents are not as judgemental, revealing that the attitudes to family life have changed as the understandings of what is permissible and appropriate have changed. This change in attitude towards family life is a fascinating sociological topic. Ingleby et al. (2014) focus more on the shared understanding of what is good and bad parenting, as opposed to looking at particular family types and assuming that these family types are ideal in themselves. The experience of childhood appears to be the critical factor, not the structure of the family. This enables us to challenge the assumption that the structure of the family determines the experience of childhood. As we have seen in this chapter, it is the relationship between parents and children that determines the experiences within the family.

We can use this argument to challenge the assumption that children who are brought up by one parent will be 'worse off' than children who are raised in a nuclear family environment. This argument is supported by Cashmere (1985), who argues that it is preferable for children to live with one 'loving' parent rather than with 'one caring and one uncaring parent'. It is important that the children receive a message that is consistent. Once more, this reinforces the argument that it is the experience of childhood that is important as opposed to the family structure.

CASE STUDY

The McNabb family are a single parent family living in the UK. They used to be a nuclear family, but the father is an alcoholic and became physically violent towards the mother and children on a regular basis. As a consequence, the mother decided to leave her husband and take the three children with her. This happened when the children were aged 9, 7 and 5 years. Although the family do not have as much income, the atmosphere in the family is very positive as Mrs McNabb and her children have a close emotional bond. Prior to leaving her husband, the children dreaded their father returning home. He would subject his wife and the children to terrifying ordeals of rage whenever he was drunk. Although the three children do not have a father in the household, they are emotionally secure. The children appear to give their mother as much emotional support as possible and they have no wish to see their father.

REFLECTIVE ACTIVITY 5.6

How will the physical, intellectual, emotional and social development of the children be affected by their circumstances?

FEEDBACK ON REFLECTIVE ACTIVITY

The children may be less affluent now that Mrs McNabb has left her husband and this might impact on their physical development, but they appear to be more content within their single parent household. They are free from Mr McNabb's drunken rages. They might not have the latest electronic learning gadgets, but they are growing up within an emotionally sound household and this enables the children the opportunity to develop intellectually. They will also find that their social skills develop within this pleasant household environment. In this example, the McNabb children may have a more positive experience of family life than if they had stayed together as a nuclear family.

DIFFERENT CULTURES AND DIFFERENT FAMILIES

Haralambos and Holborn (2008) emphasise the importance of cultural diversity and family type, of which there are a number of different forms, in the UK. This variation in family type is a possible consequence of immigration. Changes in family type can be witnessed within UK social trends. The figures show that there are differences within cultural groups in the UK. In 2009, over 50 per cent of black children in the UK were living in single parent families. This figure contrasts with Asian children as over 80 per cent of UK Asians were living with both married parents in 2009. The importance of marriage appears to vary according to culture, and this social factor appears to influence experiences of childhood in the UK. In 2015, 90 per cent of all UK males aged 15–19 years were living at home with their parents. This contrasts with 88 per cent of females. Again, cultural differences can be important as girls in Asian cultures may be married at a younger age so they do not live with their parents.

It is important to remember that family life is not 'static'. The structure of the family is influenced by individuals. Haralambos and Holborn (2008) argue that the work of Roger Ballard (1990) illustrates how emigration influences family type. Ballard's research reveals that when families move to the UK, their family structure changes in response to differing economic circumstances. The South Asian families on which Ballard completed his research saw changes in the role of women following emigration to the UK. This, in turn, impacted on the family structure, with families becoming more independent as a result of these changing economic circumstances, and extended families beyond nuclear families became less common.

CASE STUDY

Michael immigrated to England from Ireland when he was 19. His three brothers travelled with him. The brothers left Ireland because of the challenging economic circumstances in Ireland. Michael recalls that the train station they arrived at in England was larger than their whole village! Michael comes from a Catholic family, and recalls that 'his faith' was one of the most important factors in him managing to cope with such a change in his circumstances. 'The family' is a very important part of Roman Catholic culture. Although Michael and his brothers were separated from the rest of the family, they remained incredibly close emotionally as a result of their beliefs.

REFLECTIVE ACTIVITY 5.7

How is Michael's cultural background influencing his social experience of childhood?

FEEDBACK ON REFLECTIVE ACTIVITY

At times, it can be easy to take the family for granted when they are present all the time. As the saying goes, it's only when something is taken from us that we realise how important it actually is. In Michael's case, he has emigrated from another country. It is when he does not have most of his family nearby through immigrating to the UK that he comes to realise the importance of his brothers. The strong emotional bond that is shared between the brothers appears to be a strategy for coping with the difficulty of being apart from the rest of the family. In this instance, the social nature of culture is having a profound impact on Michael's experience of family.

THE CONSEQUENCES OF FAMILY SEPARATION

Family breakdown is often featured in the media. In general, family breakdown is portrayed in a negative way, as something that is not good for children. The increase in marital breakdown is considered to be a signal that the family is not as important as it used to be. The consequences of marital breakdown should not, however, be necessarily associated with family breakdown. Just because there are threats to marriage do not necessarily assume that families are breaking down. Chester (1985) studied the factors influencing the decline of marriage rates in Western countries. Chester (ibid.) writes that this decline has occurred throughout a number of Western countries including Sweden, Denmark, the UK, Germany and the USA. The research reveals that, in general, marriage has become less popular as an institution across a number of European countries. This research on Europe is supported by Haralambos and Holborn (2008) who outline that, in the UK, marriage rates have fallen in general. On the Office for National Statistics website, it is revealed that the number of single parents with dependent children rose from 1.6 million in 1997 to 2 million in 2012. These changing family trends have been anticipated for years. Joan Chandler (1991) argues that cohabitation (or living together before marriage) has become an acceptable convention.

REFLECTIVE ACTIVITY 5.8

There are some families in the UK who interpret family life in a spiritual way. Do you think that this is likely to lead to positive experiences for children and families?

FEEDBACK ON REFLECTIVE ACTIVITY

There are also some groups in UK society who associate education with religious beliefs. This can have a very positive impact for children and families. The spiritual dimension that is given to education results in belief and commitment. The same can happen if the family is viewed in a spiritual way. The family is encouraged to act out of a sense of love and spiritual commitment. This can lead to loyalty and security. This can also help the family members to develop strong social and emotional bonds. In this way, interpreting the family in a way that is spiritual can result in a positive experience of family life.

RESEARCH ACTIVITY

Ignore the saying that 'there are lies, damned lies and statistics', and visit the Office for National Statistics website and collate some statistics to support the portrayal of the UK family provided in this chapter.

THE BREAKDOWN OF MARRIAGE

Haralambos and Holborn (2008) outline three forms of marital breakdown: 'divorce', 'separation' and 'empty-shell marriages'. Divorce is 'legal separation' whereas 'separation', is living apart and accepting that the marriage is over, but there is no legal sanction that this is the case. 'Empty-shell marriage' is a term that is used for couples whose marriage exists in name only.

While the Office for National Statistics reveal that in general there has been a steady rise in divorce rates, the picture is complicated. Although the number of divorces occurring in the UK doubled between 1958 and 1969 and although the Office for National Statistics (in 2006) reveals a fourth successive yearly rise in divorce rates, the number of married couples in the UK increased between 2005 and 2015. Although the UK divorce rate is very high compared to other European countries (Haralambous and Holborn (2008) record that only Denmark had a higher divorce rate in 1990), marriage continues to remain popular. It is also important to note that it is difficult to ratify the number of instances of separation and empty-shell marriages. We can probably assume that the number of empty-shell marriages has fallen now that the stigma of separation is less pronounced than it used to be. This reflects the argument that the social understandings of relationships have changed within the UK. There appears to be an emphasis on the rights of individuals as opposed to focusing on 'social expectations'. This argument is supported by Nicky Hart (1976), who draws attention to the importance of emotional involvement between couples and the factors that influence the decision-making of married couples.

DIVORCE LAW

This impact on the family in the UK has occurred as a result of changes in the law, as obtaining a divorce is now less difficult. The law has adapted in order to allow divorce settlements. Haralambos and Holborn (2008) acknowledge that, before 1857, a private act of parliament was required to obtain a divorce. This obviously ruled out enormous sections of the population who were not able to afford such a cost. Since 1857, divorce costs have fallen and the grounds for divorce have been widened. The 1971 Divorce Reform Act defined the grounds for divorce as 'the irretrievable breakdown of the marriage'. This is an explanation for the dramatic rise in divorces in the UK since 1971. Further amendments to the UK divorce law occurred at the end of 1984, and this legislation reduced the period that a couple needed to be married before they could petition for divorce from three years to one. The legislation also made the 'behaviour of the married partners' a key factor in deciding marriage settlements. Therefore, if the behaviour of one partner was the key factor leading to the divorce, the other partner's 'liability' would be reduced in the subsequent divorce settlement.

REFLECTIVE ACTIVITY 5.9

How do you think that this rise in divorce rates influences children?

FEEDBACK ON REFLECTIVE ACTIVITY

The Office for National Statistics figures appear to show that the number of divorces is continuing to rise. In recent years in the UK, around 40 per cent of all marriages ended in divorce. Nobody is likely to regard this situation as being ideal. Many children appear to want a life that is uncomplicated – a pleasant Christmas, a family holiday, parents that love them, siblings they can play with. This is not asking too much! Divorce and the circumstances that lead to divorce appear to go against what is wished for, so we can argue that this is providing a negative experience for children. We have, however, seen that there are circumstances when divorce can be helpful for children and families. As opposed to simply staying together 'for the sake of it', it can be better for children if their parents do not live together. Rather than witnessing their parents arguing and fighting, the children are better placed in a household that is not experiencing turmoil.

CASE STUDY

The Anderson family live in an area of London that is experiencing a number of social problems. Local gangs are at 'war' with each other. The local youths are affected by drug-related issues. There is a general lack of investment in the local infrastructure, and the schools are not coping with the problems in the locality.

REFLECTIVE ACTIVITY 5.10

What would interest functionalist, interactionist and conflict theory sociologists about the Anderson family?

FEEDBACK ON REFLECTIVE ACTIVITY

We have seen in this chapter that all these sociologists are interested in the family. A first point of consideration is that the children are living in a family. Is this family a nuclear family of mum, dad and the children, or is this a single parent family? How many children are there? What are their ages? These are all questions that would be asked by the sociologists. Each group of sociologists would, however, focus on different aspects of the Anderson family.

We have seen that functionalists focus on 'the big picture'. Functionalist sociologists look at the wider social factors that are impacting on families: their interest would focus on the impact that the failing infrastructure, and the lack of investment in the area, is having on the family. These factors are leading to a key social institution, the education system, struggling to cope.

The interactionist sociologists are more interested in how individuals respond to social structures. These sociologists reveal how individuals actively create social meaning. We can argue that the problems in the local area are a combination of factors, and that there are wider social factors that need to be understood and taken into consideration. There are, of course, individuals who are generating these problems. Interactionist sociologists will be interested in these personal factors, and will ask how the individuals in the family are responding 'in their own way' to these challenging circumstances.

The conflict theory sociologists base their work on the philosophy of Marx. The UK is a capitalist country, and it is predicted that there will be a violent revolution due to the contradictions present in the economic arrangements in capitalist societies. The frustration caused by a situation where there are a few pleasant areas and many unpleasant areas in the UK will be the impetus for a violent revolution. The advantage

(Continued)

(Continued)

for you as social workers is that you can use these differing explanations of the social world to influence your professional practice. The three sociological theories provide you with an account of the social world that is based on individual and structural explanations for what is happening in society. This can enrich your professional practice because you are basing what you do on the realisation that a complex range of factors influence the lives of children and families.

CONCLUSION

In this chapter, we have explored some of the sociological interest in children. We began the chapter by outlining how our three featured perspectives can be applied to give different interpretations of the family. Functionalist sociologists are interested in how children contribute to the overall well-being of societies. Is the family a force 'for good' or does it contribute to the 'dysfunction' of a society? Just as a body has its key organs, so the family is regarded as being vital for a society. In contrast to focusing on 'the big picture', we have seen that interactionist sociologists are interested in the individuals who make up a family, as the role that individuals play in a social group can, in turn, influence wider social structures. The creativity of individuals helps to explain different family structures across time and space. Those sociologists who are influenced by conflict theory are interested in how the material circumstances of society affect families. The urban squalor and its associated problems, portrayed by Mulready, reveals some of the difficulties experienced by children and families in Victorian England. Conflict theorists propose that these circumstances were created by economic factors. Change the economy and we will see the end of poverty! The chapter has outlined that the experience of family life and childhood varies across time and space, and that there is no one consistent form of family type in all human societies. The family is influenced by a complex range of material and individual factors, and in becoming aware of the importance of these varying factors, your work as social workers will become more effective. Culture and time shape family life. We have also seen some of the challenges that exist for children and families in societies. In the UK, the rising divorce rate has had a profound impact on children and their experience of family life. It could be argued that social work has never been more necessary in view of the paradox of UK society. This is a time when we appear to have 'so much', but despite this material wealth, there appear to be large numbers of children who face challenges in their family life. The wish to have a secure family life is a simple request – delivering this request appears to be altogether more complex.

CHAPTER 6

LEARNING DISABILITIES, SOCIOLOGY AND SOCIAL WORK

INTRODUCTION

This chapter is about learning disabilities and social work. It could be argued that all of us have some sort of learning disability. We might be a professor in a prestigious university, with a pedigree as a sound academic, and yet we are not able to hold a musical note. In this example, music is a learning disability. The chapter reflects on the complexity of the term 'learning disabilities'. The content then examines the cultural context of the UK by reflecting on key legislation that has been introduced to support and include individuals with complex needs within our society. The important message of the legislation is that, although not everyone is 'the same', we are all entitled to be part of the fabric of our society.

WHAT ARE LEARNING DISABILITIES?

The term 'learning disabilities' is frequently applied to significant numbers of children in UK society. The term is usually applied to noticeable disabilities, for example not being able to read or write because of an evident disability. There are individuals who have biological, genetic reasons why they are unable to do what others in society can do. Down's syndrome is an example of a genetic disorder that results in learning disabilities for those who have this chromosomal abnormality. Learning disabilities is a complex term, and we have already argued that all of us might be in possession of particular learning disabilities. There are few multi-talented individuals who are extremely good at many different things. Within the general term 'learning disabilities', there are individuals who have 'severe learning disabilities' and those who have 'moderate learning disabilities'. Some of the individuals with Down's syndrome have more complex learning disabilities, whereas others are able to take part in paid employment. There are, in other words, levels of disability within categories of disabled people. The evolving term, 'learning disabilities' interests all of the sociologists in this book. The term is a social construction as the label 'learning disabilities' is a reaction against the bad practice that has been evident in our society as we have interacted with those who have disabilities.

The language or discourse that has been used to talk about disability has changed over time. In the book, we make reference to the work of the philosopher Foucault: this is of interest to sociologists as his philosophical work explores how discourse or conversations in society have changed over time and space. The conversations about learning disabilities have literally changed over time. The term 'disability' was previously used in ways that were not enabling, as the emphasis was placed on what could not be achieved as opposed to what could be achieved. The language of disability was previously far from complimentary, for instance the words 'idiots' and 'dunces' were applied to those in our society who were unable to do what others could do. Foucault's work demonstrates how the conversations we have about the social world have changed over time, and how the language that is used in society changes as we become aware of different interpretations of the social world. Language and discourse is also influenced by social and economic movements. The severe and brutal capitalism that is evident in the 'workhouse' is different to the 'caring capitalism' that is on display today. In this version of 'caring capitalism', the language that is used to describe categories of society is more inclusive – we no longer use the words 'idiots' or 'dunces'. Medical terminology is now applied in inclusive ways in UK society. In this book, we have previously referred to religious interpretations of 'madness' by applying Foucault's work in order to explain the changing discourse about mental illness that is evident in our society. The past interpretation of mental illness as a form of 'divine punishment' has been replaced by discourse that applies medical terminology to mental health and learning disabilities.

In answering the question, 'what are learning disabilities?' we can argue that the term 'learning disability' is an example of a social construction. The term is influenced by individuals and this will interest interactionist sociologists. The pioneering individuals who have become part of the inclusive education movement have been responsible for drawing attention to discriminatory labels such as 'idiots' and 'dunces'. The work of these individuals has led to an awareness of newer terms that are less discriminatory. The term 'learning disabilities' is a more accurate description for the needs of individuals who may be perfectly 'normal' physically, but still reveal learning needs. As opposed to an all-encompassing term, 'disability', the term 'learning disability' is helpful in this instance. How we, as a society, function with regards to those with learning disabilities interests functionalist sociologists. Learning disabilities are not simply interpreted by individuals: a collective understanding of learning disabilities has been propagated and shared across our society in order to enable us, as social workers, to work as effectively as possible. Conflict theorists are interested in the economic consequences of learning disabilities. The changing discourse that is evident in our society with regards to learning disabilities is influenced by economics. It is more effective for the economy if we can be inclusive, rather than separating sections of society away from everyone else. As social workers, we can work towards achieveing best practice if we become aware of the complex nature of the term 'learning disabilities', and, in turn, the implications that this has for our professional interaction as we become part of the delivery of social services provision.

REFLECTIVE ACTIVITY 6.1

Do you think that there are better opportunities for those who have learning disabilities today compared to 50 years ago?

FEEDBACK ON REFLECTIVE ACTIVITY

The sociological perspectives in this book draw attention to the social factors influencing the world we live in. These social circumstances result from macro social structures (for example, political and economic systems that can be beyond the influence of individuals), alongside those aspects of the social world that are influenced by individuals (for example, distinct and particular forms of culture). It can be argued that the times are better today for those individuals with learning disabilities in certain cultural contexts. In the UK, we have been influenced by a vast amount of legislation that provides those with learning disabilities with tremendous opportunities to be part of the social world that most individuals enjoy. As a result of this legislation, we can argue that the times are better today for those with learning disabilities in the UK. There are opportunities for everyone as they are protected under law, and some of the key legislation that has helped our society to become as inclusive as possible is considered later in this chapter. Our work is characterised by an inclusive approach that aims to make as many opportunities available to as many people as possible. The social, economic and individual circumstances that have enabled this sense of inclusivity interest the sociologists who are featured in this book.

CASE STUDY

Suzanne has used a wheelchair since her early years and, in addition to her physical disability, she has moderate learning disabilities with reading and mathematics. Suzanne has had a social worker working with her from an early age to support and help her growth and development. The social worker was able to establish the availability of specialist help and support throughout Suzanne's formal schooling. These learning support specialists have helped in enabling Suzanne to achieve basic reading and writing, and to do basic addition and subtraction. As a result of this help and support, Suzanne feels confident about education and training. At the age of 14, the social worker helped in finding a place for Suzanne at a Steiner school. Although Suzanne's family had to pay for her to attend this school, Suzanne's education continued to develop. The advantage of the Steiner school appeared to be an appreciation of Suzanne's academic potential. At the Steiner school, Suzanne discovered that she was especially talented at art. This enabled her to spend increasing amounts of time working on her artistic projects. The confidence provided by this successful educational experience helped Suzanne in integrating with the other students, and she saw herself as an enabled person as opposed to being someone with physical and learning disabilities.

REFLECTIVE ACTIVITY 6.2

How can conflict theory be applied to this case study?

FEEDBACK ON REFLECTIVE ACTIVITY

Conflict theorists will be interested in the material circumstances that have enabled Suzanne to have this successful experience of school. It can be argued that the 'caring capitalist' system in the UK has developed the material resources that allow the state to be inclusive. It is in the economic interests of the state to create acceptance of disabilities: the more inclusive a society is, the more opportunities there are for making economic wealth. Conflict theorists interpret Suzanne's circumstances according to this economic basis and rationale. Suzanne is regarded as being someone who is experiencing oppression. As opposed to being regarded as benefiting individuals, the laws of society are regarded as being of benefit to capitalist economies.

KEY EXAMPLES OF LEGISLATION ENABLING BEST PRACTICE IN SOCIAL WORK

This next section of the book applies the work of Ingleby et al. (2014) by outlining some of the key legislation that influences our practice as social workers when we are working with those who have learning disabilities in the UK.

The Education (Handicapped Children) Act 1970

The 1970 Education Act ended the long-standing practice of children being classified as 'uneducable'. The Act ended the assumption that children 'suffering from a disability of mind' could be classed as 'unsuitable for education at school'. For the first time in UK history, every child was entitled to an education. Discriminatory labelling, however, was still in evidence as some children were still labelled as 'Educationally Sub-Normal' (ESN). This led to them being educated in 'special schools'.

The Warnock Report (1978)

The Warnock Report (1978) had a significant impact on the integration of children with learning disabilities within mainstream schools. The report resulted from a 'Special Educational Needs Report' of the Committee of Enquiry into the Education of Handicapped Children and Young People. The Warnock Report acknowledged that children have different needs at different stages of their lives – they need support at particular times and this support is helpful for their subsequent growth and development. The report advised including children with special educational needs within mainstream education and it was envisaged that only a small minority of children would need support and facilities over and above what was already being provided. Special schools were regarded as existing to meet these needs.

In many schools in the 1970s, children with learning disabilities were segregated into separate 'educational units' for their education. Warnock recommended three ways of enabling the integration of children with learning disabilities within mainstream schools. An emphasis was placed on 'location integration' so that children with learning disabilities would be educated in 'special units' within a local school. 'Social integration' was also recommended so that, although the children were educated in a special unit within a local school, they also shared break-time and extra-curricular activities with the other students and staff in the school. 'Function integration' was also recommended. Although the children were educated in a separate unit, they also shared some of the curriculum with the other children. Warnock's work was, therefore, evidencing acceptance of the concept of 'normal' as it was recommended that children ought to be educated in 'normal' mainstream schools in order to have a uniformity of educational experiences. This is different to the inclusive practice of today and increasingly, during the 1980s and 1990s, the concept of 'normality' was questioned. It was deemed to be discriminatory to label children with learning disabilities in this way, and this came to be regarded as a denigration of their human rights. The Warnock Report was not based on complete inclusive practice for children with learning disabilities because integration was regarded to be good for some children but not for others. Nevertheless, the report did emphasise the importance of listening to parental views. The Warnock Report appreciated the value of parental knowledge and stated that this information should be used in decision-making processes. This knowledge was regarded as being vital to the decisions being made about children with learning disabilities and their educational opportunities.

The Education Act 1981

The concept of 'integration' that was established in the Warnock Report (1978) is also evident in the Education Act (1981). In addition, the Education Act (1981) takes parental views into consideration. The Act deemed that all Local Education Authorities had to ensure that every child was educated in mainstream schools subject to key criteria. A key criterion was that the views of the child's parents be taken into account. It was also recommended that integration should be based on ensuring that the child received suitable provision for their educational needs. A third key criterion emphasised the importance of ensuring that there was an efficient use of resources for children during their education. The Act met with a variety of responses that ranged from enthusiasm to resistance. The legislation is associated with unprecedented levels of bureaucracy. It can be argued that, although some inclusion followed, this was in spite of the system rather than because of it. Parents had a right of appeal but, again, in practice, this was flawed. This is because the Education Act (1981) focused on 'needs', and, as such, this policy is representative of a deficit model that adjusts to needs as opposed to embracing differences. It can be argued that the acknowledgement of the positive possibilities of inclusion is absent from this legislation (Ingleby et al. 2014).

United Nations Convention on the Rights of the Child (UNCRC) (1989)

The rights of all children are established in law and enshrined in the United Nations Convention on the Rights of the Child (UN 1989). A child is defined as a person up to the age of 18. The aim of the legislation is to give equality of opportunity to all children across the world and to ensure that every child is safe, healthy and happy. It is stated in law that governments must ensure that children do not experience discrimination and that they have a right 'to an education, to be healthy, to a childhood, to be treated fairly and to be heard' (UNICEF online, cited in Ingleby et al. 2014). One of the key aims of the legislation is to make children a key part of the policies of the member states. This is particularly helpful for developing the rights of children who have learning disabilities. In exemplifying this point, improving disability access is associated with this legislation. The legislation aims at ensuring the well-being of every child in order to develop ability and potential. There are some key goals within the legislation that have helped children with learning disabilities. The United Kingdom ratified the Convention in 1991 and accepted the responsibility to implement and support actions that would help children with learning disabilities. In excess of 190 countries, including the UK, signed up to the Convention and ratified the articles (Ingleby et al. 2014). Somalia, South Sudan and the USA signed the convention but it was not ratified. South Sudan and Somalia have ratified the convention fairly recently (2013) and the USA declared its intent to do so under the Obama Administration (Ingleby et al. 2014). The importance of the legislation can be seen, as UNICEF (United Nations Children's Fund) declared 2014 as the 'Year for Innovation for Equality'. Within the legislation, Article 2 is a key statement for children with learning disabilities, with the emphasis that children should not experience any form of discrimination. The Convention is designed to apply to everyone, regardless of ethnicity, gender, religion and abilities. Article 23 relates to a child's right to full social integration and independent development, and this theme is used by the United Nations Committee on the Rights of the Child as its guiding principle for inclusion. The Convention also recognises that children are not a commodity or the property of their parents, and that they should not be regarded as 'helpless' as they are individuals with rights and 'with a voice' (Ingleby et al. 2014). Children are regarded as having the same fundamental rights as adults. The Convention is the means of achieving this key goal so the rights of children with learning disabilities are enshrined in international law. The legislation aims at sustaining and improving the lives of children worldwide. The countries that have signed up to the agreement have to bring their policy and practice in line with the aims and standards of the Convention. It is through this obligation that childrens' lives can be improved. It is, however, important to note that not only do governments promote and adhere to the Convention, but those societies and nations embrace this important legislation in order to celebrate the rights of the child (Ingleby et al. 2014).

The Education Act 1993

The Audit Commission reviewed the effectiveness of the implementation processes of the 1981 Education Act in 1992. The Commission concluded that inspection procedures were not effective and, as a result, were flawed. The 1993 Education Act attempted to improve these areas so that a stronger voice was given to parents during the education of their children. Whilst the three conditions linked to the 1981 legislation remained in place, an essential element of this new legislation saw the addition of the key phrase 'unless it is incompatible with the wishes of the parents'. This illustrates the rising importance of parental voices in the education of children, and is signignificant as it allows for the enabling of parental influence during the education of children with special educational needs (Ingleby et al. 2014).

The 1994 Salamanca Statement

This is a particularly influential international document as the content has become the catalyst for much of the educational policy aimed at delivering inclusive practice in schools in the UK (Ingleby et al. 2014). The statement was delivered at the World Conference on Special Needs and was a reaffirmation by 92 governments and 25 organisations of their commitment to 'Education for All'. This is particularly important for children with learning disabilities. The conference adopted two key documents: 'The Salamanca Statement on Principles, Policy and Practice in Special Needs Education' and 'A Framework for Action'. The statements embrace the concept that societies should work towards inclusivity and that schools are regarded as being the key environments for delivering and supporting an inclusive society. Statement 2 of the Salamanca Agreement outlines a commitment to ensuring that every child has a fundamental right to education so that they are provided with the opportunity to achieve and maintain an acceptable level of learning. The acknowledgement of the unique characteristics, interests, abilities and learning needs of each child is also enshrined within the legislation. Education systems should be designed, taking into account the wide diversity of the human world. This enables children with special educational needs to become included within 'regular schools' that are accommodated within a child-centred pedagogy that is capable of meeting these needs. These regular schools need to ensure that discriminatory attitudes are challenged, and that they provide a means of developing 'welcoming communities' that are supportive of an inclusive society and committed to achieving education for all (Ingleby et al. 2014). These schools must provide an effective education for children so that 'the efficiency and the cost-effectiveness of the entire education system' is ensured (Article 2, Salamanca Statement, 1994, cited in Ingleby et al. 2014).

The Statement requires that all governments give the highest priority to improving education systems so that they become inclusive for all children, regardless of individual differences or difficulties. The emphasis is on enabling the principle of inclusive education so that all children are fully included in the education and activities within their school, unless there are 'compelling reasons for doing otherwise' (Article 3, Salamanca Statement, 1994, cited in Ingleby et al. 2014). In the final statement in Article 2, there is recognition of the principle that inclusive policy should achieve effective education for the majority of children. The implications are that the needs of most children are best served through this policy. The Statement also specifically recognises the role of the parents in their child's education and that their involvement in the decision-making process must be encouraged and facilitated (Ingleby et al. 2014). This change is a consequence of the actions of 'pressure groups, parents and other supporters' (ibid p 130).

The 1997 Green Paper: *Excellence for All Children*

In the 1997 Green Paper policy document, *Excellence for All Children*, the Education and Employment Minister, David Blunkett, draws attention to the important principle of ensuring that children with special educational needs (SEN) are included formally within mainstream education. Blunkett states that:

while recognising the paramount importance of meeting the needs of individual children, and the necessity of specialist provision for some, we shall promote the inclusion of children with SEN within mainstream schooling wherever possible. We shall remove barriers which get in the way of meeting the needs of all children and re-define the role of special schools to develop a network of specialist support. (DfEE 1997, p5)

Special Educational Needs and Disability Act 2001 (SENDA)

The Special Educational Needs and Disability Act (SENDA) (2001) 'Part 1' strengthened the growing importance of inclusive education by drawing attention to the importance of radical and inclusive approaches to school design. The Act attempted to address issues within the 1996 Education Act by strengthening the right to receive mainstream schooling. Two conditions are associated with the legislation: that disabled children can only go to mainstream schools on condition that this is compatible with their parents' wishes, and that the education of the other children is effective (Ingleby et al. 2014). A revised code of practice on SEN came into effect in 2002, based on the SENDA principles and incorporating the new SEN regulations, and this made inclusion a legal requirement.

The Education Act 1996

The Education Act 1996 represents another important development in the UK's establishment of education and inclusivity. A key element of the legislation ensured that local authorities educated all children in mainstream schools, unless this was not possible because of resource issues or because this was opposed to the wishes of the parents.

Evaluating Educational Inclusion (2000)

In *Evaluating Educational Inclusion* (Ofsted 2000) we see an understanding of inclusion that was far broader than merely meeting educational needs. The emphasis was placed on ensuring 'equal opportunities for all pupils, whatever their age, gender, ethnicity, attainment and background' (Ingleby et al. 2014, p132).

Special Educational Needs: a New Look (2010)

In *Special Educational Needs: A New Look* (2010), Baroness Warnock revisited the argument on inclusion. The content of the document reconsidered both inclusion and statementing (in other words, the formal documenting of special needs) by arguing that the number of statements had been far in excess of what had ever been envisaged. Warnock recommended an approach to inclusion that was based on meeting the diverse needs of the child. Although Warnock's approach was criticised because some of the data appeared to be 'dated', the argument that issues with resourcing SEN and the bureaucracy that is associated with SEN were accepted as being mitigating factors.

Every Child Matters (ECM) (2003) and Early Years Foundation Stage (EYFS)

The main focus areas of 'Every Child Matters' (ECM) was early intervention, a shared sense of responsibility, information sharing and integrated front-line services. The Early Years Foundation Stage (EYFS) linked to the ECM agenda by helping all children to achieve the five principles of Every Child Matters: staying safe, staying healthy, enjoying and achieving, being able to make an eventual economic contribution and making a positive contribution to society. The EYFS is based on principles of: 'equality of opportunity and anti-discriminatory practice and ensuring that every child is included and not disadvantaged because of ethnicity, culture or religion, home language, family background, learning difficulties or disabilities, gender or ability' (EYFS, n.d.)

Statutory Framework for the Early Years Foundation Stage 2017

The Early Years Framework was revised in 2012, following recommendations from the Tickell Review in 2011. The reforms were intended to reduce paperwork and bureaucracy so that partnerships between parents and professionals could be strengthened. The four guiding principles recognised that each child is unique and that 'positive relationships' must be provided within an enabling environment. There is the recognition that children learn in different ways and at different rates. This reveals that our society and its education system have changed over the years and that the education of all children ideally results in the integration of every child in order to realise inclusive practice. An inclusive society is evidenced by a series of inclusive educational policies. The ideal of 'including all children' is, however, a challenge. Including children with learning disabilities remains at the forefront of inclusive education but the practicalities of realising this ideal are not straightforward. Although the governments of the UK have made clear statements regarding inclusion, the challenges of policy and practice remain (Ingleby et al. 2014).

INCLUDING THOSE WITH LEARNING DISABILITIES WITHIN A DIVERSE SOCIETY

Increasingly, the inclusion of children with learning disabilities has come to be recognised as more than just addressing special educational needs. Although the groups of children listed within the concept of 'inclusion' are defined by their cultural and physical abilities, it is wrong to confine diversity only to race and culture (Ingleby et al. 2014). The challenge in applying inclusion to children with learning disabilities is based on ensuring that all children are included in activities whenever this is possible.

The understanding of inclusion with regards to children with learning disabilities has moved from a medical interpretation to a social model. This has occurred because of changes in legislation that have had an impact on the curriculum. The medical understanding of children with learning disabilities is rigid, and criteria appear to be fixed and determined (ibid.). In contrast, the social model appears to be based on a more flexible understanding of learning disabilities. Identity is regarded as being socially constructed and the differences within cultural groups are celebrated and embraced. However, although the medical model does not require society to change, the social model of learning disabilities is dependent on those in society being prepared and willing to change. This is reflected in the international agreements on learning disabilities, especially in the last two decades. The assertion is that working with children with learning disabilities is based on an on-going evolutionary ideal that societies must work towards. The medical and social models are based on placing an emphasis on disability, but good social work practice with children with learning disabilities should be based on enabling diversity (ibid.).

In the Ofsted report *Evaluating Educational Inclusion* (Ofsted 2000), a wider view of inclusion is embraced. Educational inclusion is regarded to be more than a concern about any one group of children (for example, those children who have been or are likely to be excluded from school). The scope of inclusion in this report is broad. The important basis of the report is 'equal opportunities for all children', regardless of their age, gender, ethnicity, attainment or background. The report pays particular attention to the provision that is being made for different groups of children within schools. The term 'different groups' applies to: girls and boys; minority ethnic and faith groups; travellers, asylum seekers and refugees; children who need support to learn English as an additional language (EAL); children with special educational needs; gifted and talented pupils; children 'looked after' by the local authority; sick children; and any other children who are at risk of disaffection and exclusion (ibid., p4).

In 2000, a toolkit of materials was developed to help children with learning disabilities (*Index for Inclusion: Developing Learning and Participation in Schools*, Booth and Ainscow 2002). This resource was made available to every school and Local Education Authority in the UK. The intention behind the production of this resource was to help and support the development of inclusive practice in schools, and the aim was to enable all pupils to participate as fully as possible by removing the barriers to their participation in learning (Ingleby et al. 2014). The toolkit was published by the Centre for Studies on Inclusive Education (CSIE), which emphasised the importance of 'building supportive communities and fostering high achievement for all staff and students' (Booth and Ainscow 2000, cited in Das and Das 2010, p131). The materials were intended to enable settings to 'adopt a self-review approach to analyse their cultures, policies and practices and to identify the barriers to learning and participation'

(Booth and Ainscow 2000, cited in Das and Das 2010, p131). This approach to inclusion is based on a social model interpretation of children with learning disabilities. The toolkit provides a range of inclusive ideals, including valuing all students and staff, increasing participation in the curriculum and recognising that inclusion in education is linked to inclusion in society (Ingleby et al. 2014).

THE FACTORS THAT CONTRIBUTE TO DIVERSITY

There are many factors that contribute to diversity and inclusivity. Extrinsic and intrinsic factors are especially important. Extrinsic factors (conditioning or determining factors) include: nationality; geography, or where the child lives; economic impact, for example poverty; household income; culture and ethnicity; and social factors relating to class, family and background. The intrinsic factors (that are individual or specific) include physical and genetic factors; health; social and emotional well-being; and cognitive abilities.

THE EMPLOYABILITY AGENDA

Although the emergence of the inclusive agenda can be tracked through changes in legislation, guidance and policy at both national and international levels, there are barriers to its effective delivery. Devarakonda (2013) argues that it is important to acknowledge that changes to policy occur during policy-making processes. In addition, a lack of awareness of the social issues around inclusive practice will have a profound impact on children and families. This impact could be reduced by encouraging reflective practice that is based on the constant reappraisal of professional work with children who have learning disabilities. It should also be acknowledged that practitioners are part of society and there is, therefore, the challenge of avoiding prejudices and perceptions. There exist assumptions about certain social groups in societies and this creates 'barriers to the provision of equal opportunities for children in these groups' (Tedam 2009, p123).

THE PARENTS AS PARTNERS AGENDA

The UN Convention highlights the importance of the family's role in the lives of its children. Throughout our developing understanding of the value of inclusive practice both in society and in education, the involvement and voice of both children and parents is central. This principle is embraced in the Early Years Foundation Document, where partnership with parents is recognised as a key element in making effective progress when we are working with children who have learning disabilities. Parents are children's first and most enduring educators. When parents and practitioners work together, it is argued that 'the results have a positive impact on children's development and learning' (EYFS, n.d.). The document also states that the diversity of the individual children and communities should be respected and that no family or child should experience discrimination. In the EYFS, the need to work in partnership with parents is clearly stated. The concept of planning for the needs of the individual child is cited and specific reference is made to inclusive practice in the stated aim involving equality of opportunity. The EYFS seeks to provide quality and consistency in all early years settings, so that every child makes good progress and no child gets left behind. The legislation aims to provide a secure foundation through learning and development opportunities which are planned around the needs and interests of each individual child, which are assessed and reviewed regularly. An emphasis is placed on enabling partnership working between practitioners, parents and carers, equality of opportunity and anti-discriminatory practice in order to ensure that every child is included and supported (EYFS 2007, p2, cited in Ingleby et al. 2014).

This 'framework' is based on the important principle that every child is unique. Fitzgerald (2004, p21) argues that all parties need to have a shared understanding of what partnership means to them in order to work effectively together, and that: 'for partnerships to be maintained, it is vital that there are effective strategies in place to facilitate two-directional communication and support'.

KEY PRINCIPLES OF WORKING IN PARTNERSHIP WITHIN LEARNING DISABILITIES

It is important for social workers who are working with parents to focus on the family and the children so that they are treated with respect. It is, therefore, useful to base our work on a number of key guiding principles. We need to ensure that we respect children as diverse individuals and that we are also fully aware of the many ways that parents demonstrate love and care for their children. This helps us in communicating effectively with children and parents in diverse ways. Our practice as social workers, when we are working with families who have children with learning disabilities, must be based on respect for parents' decisions about their own lives. It is important to ensure that we are committed to communicating on a regular basis in a courteous manner. We need to ensure that we listen to parents' views about our work so that we can act on their wishes, when this is helpful. It is also essential to acknowledge that there are different views about childhood, child-rearing practices, learning goals, roles of parents and roles of social workers. Good social work practice is based on clear communication about ways in which we can help each other as we work together in partnership. This good practice will be based on clear communication channels for parents and practitioners so that we are able to explain to others the records, procedures and actions that are undertaken in our social work practice. It is important that we base our practice on recognising that there are different cultural values so that we consider these differences with an open mind. Our partnership with other social workers, other agencies and parents will be enhanced if we take these principles into consideration.

INCLUSIVE SETTINGS

'Difference is of interest to children, and the recognition of difference as positive rather than negative is an important aim for early childhood professionals' (Nutbrown et al. 2013, p13). Inclusive settings focus on supporting the positive aspects of difference and attempting to remove the barriers that prevent children from progressing or accessing opportunities. The social benefits of an inclusive setting are significant. When settings are characterised by diversity, this helps social workers to promote best practice. Accepting others in view of their gender, cultural differences, class, income and ethnicity informs the development of best professional practice. 'It is equally important to acknowledge that inclusion also benefits children without disabilities. When placed in inclusive settings, young children are more accepting of children with disabilities' (Vakil et al. 2003, p187).

INCLUSIVE PRACTICE AND THE ROLE OF THE SOCIAL WORKER

The concept of 'inclusive play' is as elusive as the term 'inclusion' in that there is no agreed definition that is set in stone. This is in itself, therefore, a challenge to social workers. In England, the EYFS regards an enabling environment as one of the overarching principles of good professional practice as 'children learn and develop well in enabling environments, in which their experiences respond to their individual needs and there is a strong partnership between practitioners and parents and/or carers' (EYFS n.d., p3). It is important for social workers to provide an enabling environment in order to support the inclusive play that will help children to grow and develop. The environment can be changed to meet diverse needs and promote the opportunities for children to investigate, experiment, role-play, socially interact with their peers and much more (Ingleby et al. 2014). It is important, as social workers, to be open to exploring a variety of sensory approaches as this also accommodates diversity. 'A rich play environment creates opportunities for children to follow a number of paths through their explorations and discoveries to open-ended destinations' (Casey, 2010, p21). The richer the environment, in terms of the stimulation that is being offered, the greater is the possibility that the children will be able to learn and develop. When children are at play in this environment, the practitioner can use these opportunities to observe the child in order to become more aware of how to intervene as a social worker. Social workers need to ensure that they respond effectively to the individual child's needs. Effective social work practice will ensure that children develop an understanding of the meaning of inclusive play. A key element of this 'good practice' results in practitioners developing an understanding of childrens' perceptions of them. The differences that exist in individuals and between social groups ought to be embraced as opposed to being ignored (Ingleby et al. 2014). The emphasis is not so much on changing the child, but on providing an enabling environment that allows children to flourish and develop. This practice is based on encouraging high aspirations for all children so that we can avoid homogenising them – social workers should not attempt to make all the children the same! At times, this is a difficult agenda as our professional practice can be based on challenging society's preconceptions. The responsibility of social workers in enabling good inclusive practice is, therefore, more than just a commitment to the child, but, indeed, a commitment to an ideology of society. Society, in turn, needs to be committed to the concept of inclusive practice. To enable this symbiotic relationship involves social, moral and ethical choices. It is a question of upholding and maintaining childrens' rights – their right for respect so that the children are treated with equal value (Ingleby et al. 2014). Education needs to be adapted to children so that our work as social workers is based on exploring the possibilities rather than the limitations.

INCLUSION: AN ON–GOING CHALLENGE

Inclusion remains an on-going challenge for social workers. There is within social work a difficulty in meeting all the agendas that we are asked to meet in our professional practice. We are asked to raise attainment and meet specific targets within a pre-determined time frame. We are also asked to embrace differences and provide opportunities to support children and yet our work may be undone in the wider environment. These are challenges for us as social workers. The agenda may also become complicated due to government priorities that are frequently based on meeting targets. In this instance, accountability for attainment does not relate to the challenges that are associated with realising inclusion. In addition, an increasingly restricted curriculum, again related to levels and targets, presents challenges for us as social workers. It is also important to note that the lack of a clear, agreed definition for inclusion is problematic. To know if inclusion is effective requires consensus about both the terminology and the criteria upon which to judge its success. Whilst the key to success is often linked to early identification and intervention, how do we know that this will be successful in the long term (Ingleby et al. 2014)? The fact that inclusion is at least on the agenda, that it is debated and that society does support the principle of ensuring children's rights, is a positive move in the right direction. Inclusion remains an on-going process – a constant striving for the ideal developmental conditions for children with learning disabilities.

CONCLUSION

This chapter has explored how our professional practice as social workers can be enhanced when we are working with children who have learning disabilities. At the beginning of the chapter, we showed that the term 'learning disabilities' is complex – we all have some sort of learning disability! We have also seen that the understanding of learning disabilities is complex. There are medical and social models of disability, and each of these models interprets learning disabilities in different ways. The scientific understanding of learning disabilities is based on accepting the importance of Western medicine, whereas the social model of learning disabilities draws attention to the social circumstances that change perceptions of learning disabilities. The chapter has outlined how the concept of inclusion has become a critical part of UK society. We have explored the consequences of some of the key legislation that has been introduced to UK society in order to develop best practice with children who have learning disabilities. UK society is based on important principles of diversity and inclusion. This 'best practice' is not based on a view that everyone is 'the same', however the view is that everyone is entitled to the same. At times, it is difficult to realise this vision of an inclusive society: there are pressures from governments and their agendas, and there are the social pressures of poverty, disease, unemployment and crime. To our best abilities, however, we are working towards this agenda in our professional practice as social workers with children who have learning disabilities. If we base our professional practice on the important principle of inclusion, we are able to say that we are doing everything we can in order to ensure that we are creating as inclusive a society as possible. Surely, there can be no finer principle?

CHAPTER 7

MENTAL HEALTH, SOCIOLOGY AND SOCIAL WORK

INTRODUCTION

'Don't worry!' the nurse grinned at me. 'Their first time everyone's scared to death.' I tried to smile but my skin was tight like parchment. Doctor Gordon fitted two metal plates on the side of my head. He gave me a wire to bite. I shut my eyes. There was a brief silence, like an in-drawn breath. Then something bent down and shook me like the end of the world. 'Wheee-wheee-wheee!' it shrilled, through an air of crackling blue light and with each flash a great bolt drubbed me till I thought my bones would break and the sap fly out of them like a split plant. (Plath, 1963, p151)

All of us here are like rabbits hippity hopping through our Walt Disney World. We're not here because we're rabbits. We'd be rabbits wherever we were. We're here because we can't adjust to our rabbit hood. We need a good strong wolf like the nurse to teach us our place. (Kesey 1962, p55)

The two quotations from the authors Sylvia Plath and Ken Kesey highlight concerns that have existed over mental illness in the West. Some academics (for example, Thomas Scheff) have drawn attention to the controversy that is present in this area of health and care. There is even a question as to whether or not mental illness actually exists. The argument runs that mental illnesses are forms of deviant behaviour, and the behaviour of those who are mentally ill is troubling for the social order.

This requires intervention and control. This theme will be explored in this chapter. Mental health is a key area of social work. In order to develop our professional work as social workers in this area, it is important to reflect on what sociologists are interested in when they consider the nature of mental illness.

FUNCTIONALIST INTEREST IN MENTAL ILLNESS

We have seen that functionalists are interested in wider social factors. With mental illness, they consider the social organisation of health systems. Functionalists regard key social organisations as similar to the vital part that key organs play in the human body. The health system of a social group is visualised as being akin to the role that the heart plays in the body – as long as the heart remains healthy, so the body functions effectively. Similarly, as long as the health system of a social group is effective, so that social group can function efficiently. Functionalist sociologists are also interested in the ways in which understandings of mental illness have changed in societies over time. A number of social scientists have reflected on changing interpretations of mental illness to outline the social factors that influence our understanding of the mentally ill. Hirst and Woolley (1982) apply the work of the French philosopher Foucault in order to demonstrate how wider social structures change and, in turn, impact on our understanding of mental illness. Hirst and Woolley reveal that, in societies such as England's, there has been a change in perceptions of what contributes to mental health and well-being. In Victorian England, religious explanations were applied in order to help understand mental illness. The mentally ill were literally removed from society and placed in asylums – institutions that were isolated from the rest of society. The mentally ill and their families were regarded as being punished by God for some kind of transgression against 'his divine law'. Hirst and Woolley (ibid.) reveal that, over time, this social interpretation of mental illness changes in societies such as the UK's. Through the nineteenth century, a scientific interpretation of mental illness replaces this religious explanation. There emerges a medical model of mental illness: Hirst and Woolley suggest that this medical model depends on a particular train of thought. 'Condition A' is expected to respond to 'Treatment A' and to improve. The challenge with many mental illnesses appears to be that they do not respond to this course of action. In the quotation from Plath, her treatment sounds more like something you would experience upon being tortured! The problem for the doctors and nurses treating mental illnesses is that the illness does not appear to improve following this medical model of care. Hirst and Woolley (1982) outline which social factors influence mental health and this is of interest to functionalist sociologists. Mental illness is reinterpreted, and we see the emergence of 'care in the community' in the UK in response to a failing set of arrangements for the mentally ill. The asylums are closed and a new form of treatment is offered that appears to be less punitive and more humane. The critical factor in these changes is not so much the 'illness', but the social understanding of mental illness.

INTERACTIONIST INTEREST IN MENTAL ILLNESS

Earlier in the book, we have argued that interactionists trace their approach to sociology back to philosophers such as Kant. Audi (1999) suggests that these philosophers place their emphasis on how individuals interpret the world that they frequent. Interactionist sociologists are more interested in the individual perceptions of mental illness. As opposed to 'solving mental illness', the individual experiences of mental illness are considered. Interactionist sociologists study the personal accounts of mental illness, like the reflections given by Plath and Kesey. There is a belief that such reflections reveal the reality of mental illness. Our Western medical model has not found a cure for mental illnesses, and if we apply the work of Kant, we can argue that this is because it is impossible to find a cure to something that is so complex and so challenging. In understanding mental illness, we need to focus instead on the perceptions and experiences of those who are dealing with it. Plath (1963) writes about mental illness in a powerful way. We witness the struggle that she is experiencing in her world. Interactionist sociologists are interested in this sense of personal experience. It is argued that this is where the 'reality' of the social world rests. The individual experiences of those with mental illnesses and the expression of these experiences in literature, art and music give a critical insight into the reality of mental illness, according to interactionist sociologists. If we look at the complexity of mental illness in the UK, we can argue that this approach is fundamentally correct. The medical approach of providing 'Treatment A' for 'Condition B' does not appear to have worked. This reveals that there is not a convincing scientific procedure for treating mental illnesses. We can learn much from the reflections of authors such as Plath and Kesey. Both authors reveal how individuals influence the understanding of mental illness. In *One Flew Over the Cuckoo's Nest*, the leading protagonist in the novel shapes understandings of mental illness through the creative force of his personality. In a famous scene in the novel, Randle McMurphy organises an illegal boat trip for residents incarcerated in an asylum. Although the owner of the boat appears to be uneasy about those who are going on the boat trip, he is convinced by McMurphy that all the crew are from an academic research institute. The 'weird' perception of academics that appears to exist within the wider community convinces the boat owner that these mentally ill individuals are actually eminent researchers! This proves the interactionist argument that individuals create social reality. This is especially true with mental illness when there is no precise definition of what exactly mental illnesses are.

CONFLICT THEORY AND MENTAL ILLNESS

Conflict theorists are interested in the economy and how economic forces influence social life. The theory is based on the argument that capitalist societies are based on contradictions, for example a relatively small group of individuals own the majority of the resources in capitalist societies. It is considered that contradictions like this result in conflict in capitalist societies, and that this tension will eventually lead to a social revolution. Conflict theorists have been proven correct: there have been revolutions in Russia and China among many other places. Capitalism has been replaced with communism in some societies, the principle within communism being that everything is equally divided between the population. This is considered to be a state of social utopia. Conflict theorists assert that there are more mental health problems in societies that are based on capitalism, as the inequalities in capitalism will lead to neuroses and psychoses in individuals. Neuroses are understood to be mild disorders of mental health. Mild anxieties are more likely in capitalist societies for the workers because of insecurity of pay and temporary contracts of employment. There is a lack of job security, not enough money to live a comfortable life and working conditions are not good. These economic conditions can lead to neuroses in working people. The inequalities in capitalist societies result in the wealthy elite being looked after and the majority of the population struggling to survive. There is not a health system that is accessible to all the population – health services are confined to the wealthy elite. For those individuals who have psychoses, or more severe mental illnesses, there is nothing to help them. They are likely to become a danger to wider society and experience eventual incarceration.

Conflict theorists are interested in other societies with different social arrangements. It is assumed that societies not based on capitalism will have a lower rate of mental illness. Societies that have not experienced an industrial revolution have not got working conditions like capitalist societies because the means of production are distributed more fairly and there is less tension between social groups. In these more equalitarian societies, there is likely to be less mental illness. These assumptions come from the philosophy of Marx, and academics influenced by conflict theory will be interested in exploring the strengths and weaknesses of these assumptions. The academic debate considers questions such as: Are non-capitalist societies free from mental illness? Does capitalism result in more mental illness? Do communist societies address the needs of the mentally ill? These three questions are based on the assumption that there is such a thing as mental illness. If we combine conflict theory with the other two sociological perspectives, we get an interesting research focus. This is the platform upon which we consider the rest of the focus of this chapter. There are a number of interesting issues that are associated with mental illness, and we will reflect on these issues by considering how functionalist, interactionist and conflict theorist sociologists help us to think about mental illnesses in ways that are beneficial for social work.

A DEFINITION OF MENTAL ILLNESS

REFLECTIVE ACTIVITY 7.1

How can we define mental illness and mental illnesses?

FEEDBACK ON REFLECTIVE ACTIVITY

In this chapter, we have already seen some of the challenges associated with mental health and well-being. We have referred to 'mental illness' and 'mental illnesses'. Are both of these terms appropriate? Can we refer to 'mental illness' in entirety or are there 'mental illnesses'? There are a number of ways of explaining mental illnesses. We can assume that there is actually an illness in the Western medical sense of the term. In other words, there is something wrong with the person and a cure can be found. The problem with understanding mental illnesses in this way is that there are many examples of mental illness that don't fit into this train of thought. There is not a pill that can be given to a schizophrenic that stops that person from being a schizophrenic. There is an argument that mental illnesses are just forms of deviant behaviour. The behaviour goes against social conventions and it offers a threat to the social norm. However, much deviant behaviour, like crime, is based on choice, and who would choose to be mentally ill? So, it is not appropriate to define mental illness as deviance in many instances. Mental illness appears to be a state of mind that is not fully understood. As time passes, however, it is possible that we will gain more insight into the causes of mental illnesses. We just need to accept that, currently, we do not have all the answers to the question of mental illness as yet.

DEBATES ABOUT DEFINITIONS OF MENTAL ILLNESS IN SOCIAL SCIENCE

The argument that mental illness is deviant behaviour interests social scientists for a number of reasons (Ingleby 2010), and there are two specific compelling reasons for this notion. In the first instance, if we understand mental illness to be deviance, this simplifies what mental illnesses are. In the second instance, we get an umbrella term that covers all mental illnesses, that is to say, they are all perceived as examples of deviant behaviour (ibid.). This builds on the understanding that there exist forms of 'normal' and 'abnormal' behaviour that are shared across societies. This large-scale focus appeals to functionalist understandings of societies. The terms 'abnormal' and 'normal' are, however, problematic.

REFLECTIVE ACTIVITY 7.2

What is abnormal behaviour?

FEEDBACK ON REFLECTIVE ACTIVITY

Abnormal behaviour can be defined as behaviour that is not conventional. The creativity of individuals in a social group can be 'abnormal', and this creative abnormality fascinates interactionist sociologists. Golightley (2004) argues that there are different types of abnormal behaviour: behaviour that deviates from statistical and social norms; behaviour that is maladaptive and thus produces negative consequences; and behaviour that produces feelings of personal distress. The next section of the chapter amplifies these examples of abnormal behaviour.

Behaviour that differs from a statistical norm

This form of abnormal behaviour is presented using descriptive statistics via quantifiable research approaches. The majority of the population are perceived to eat breakfast, lunch and dinner as their main meals each day. If we use this definition of normality, anyone eating significantly less or significantly more than this is perceived as being 'abnormal'. There are, however, problems with this definition of abnormality. What about the person with diabetes, who is advised to eat little and often? Are they 'abnormal' because most people in society are not doing this?

Behaviour that differs from the social norms

Abnormal behaviour may be measured by the social norms or conventions in society. The 'abnormal' goes against these established conventions. Once again, there are difficulties with this understanding of abnormality. What is considered to be abnormal differs according to time and place. To exemplify this argument, worshipping God in church was at one time generally considered to be normal behaviour. In contemporary societies such as the UK's, there are many people who do not go to church to worship God. What was once normal behaviour is not necessarily a social norm today.

Behaviour that is maladaptive

This explanation of abnormality considers that behaviour that produces negative effects for the social group is abnormal. According to this understanding of abnormality, violence is regarded as being abnormal because of its harmful effects on society. It is the emphasis placed on the maladaptive nature of the behaviour that distinguishes this definition from those of the previous two categories. This definition of abnormality is also problematic: there are accepted forms of violence in many societies, and we could argue that the armed forces in any nation represent the social acceptance of violence.

Feelings of personal distress

This definition of abnormality considers that abnormal behaviour is a product of personal distress. If we inflict mental cruelty on someone, this could be perceived as abnormal behaviour as it causes personal distress to another person. Again, however, there are problems with this understanding of abnormality. In some societies, there are socially sanctioned 'interrogators' who are experts in the creation of mental distress. These individuals are asked to 'get to the truth' in their official role as state interrogators.

All of these definitions of abnormality are problematic. This indicates that if we consider mental illness to be a form of abnormal behaviour, we are also likely to experience difficulties in establishing a suitable working definition for what we are trying to understand. To expand on this argument further, let us reflect on normal behaviour. Ingleby (2010) argues that normal behaviour demonstrates the following characteristics. If something is normal, it is considered to be based on an accurate perception of reality. Normal behavior can be regarded as imitating what others do so that we become socially acceptable. It can be regarded as constraining involuntary urges so that we have a sense of self-worth and are capable of productive behaviour.

We can, however, argue that this understanding of what is normal is actually ideal behaviour. Moreover, normal behaviour is understood in relation to what is abnormal. Perhaps both forms of behaviour are present in most individuals, to a lesser or greater extent? Perhaps it is only an excess of abnormal behaviour that is problematic? This, in turn, means that if we are able to understand what it is like to be 'abnormal', how can we ever claim to be completely 'normal' (Ingleby 2010)?!

CLASSIFICATIONS OF MENTAL ILLNESS

The previous section reveals how difficult it is to define what is 'normal' and 'abnormal'. Defining mental illness can be just as complicated. To help our understanding of this 'complex'? area, let us reflect on what we do know about mental illnesses.

Neuroses and psychoses

In Western cultures, we have come to classify types of mental illnesses. There is a two-fold classification of 'neuroses' and 'psychoses'. A neurosis is a mild form of mental illness. A neurotic person knows that they are behaving in an unusual way. In contrast, a psychotic person is not aware that they are behaving abnormally. For example, someone suffering from an obsessive–compulsive disorder in which they find themselves continually washing their hands is aware that this is not a 'normal' thing to do.

In psychotic behaviour, this awareness of abnormality is less apparent. In effect, there is a loss of reality. As a consequence, the behaviour is not regarded as 'strange'. It is regarded as being perfectly normal behaviour, based on the reality of their world.

REFLECTIVE ACTIVITY 7.3

If you are working with someone with schizophrenia, what are some of the challenges? How can sociology help your practical social work?

FEEDBACK ON REFLECTIVE ACTIVITY

Schizophrenia is colloquially understood as the presence of a 'split mind'. This form of mental illness poses many challenges, and there are likely to be challenging forms of behaviour. Schizophrenia can manifest as 'voices in the head', which, in turn, can produce behaviour that is volatile and unpredictable. In view of this, it can be difficult to have a consistent relationship with someone who suffers from schizophrenia. Our three sociological models draw attention to the social conditions influencing understandings of schizophrenia. We have seen with functionalism that these understandings change as social circumstances change. We have also seen how the interactionists draw attention to the individual experiences of mental illnesses such as schizophrenia. The response to schizophrenia can also depend on the wider economic infrastructure as experienced by the individual.

It is important to note that there are particular differences between neurotic and psychotic disorders. Neurotic disorders include anxiety, phobias, obsessive behaviour, some forms of depression and psychosomatic disorders (physical symptoms that have no apparent physical cause). In contrast, the psychoses include schizophrenia and forms of complex depression that are long-lasting and debilitating (Ingleby 2010). We can begin to understand mental illness by appreciating the differences that exist between neuroses and psychoses. We can then attempt to classify other forms of mental illnesses, keeping in mind the social factors that influence the experience of mental illness.

RESEARCH ACTIVITY

Carry out some internet research on schizophrenia. Complete a word search in order to obtain more information about this form of mental illness.

REFLECTIVE ACTIVITY 7.4

In the disorder 'Munchausen's syndrome', individuals believe that they have acute illnesses and habitually present themselves for hospital treatment. The 'patient' is able to provide plausible evidence for having the disorder but this is false. Do you think that this is an example of 'neurotic' or 'psychotic' behaviour?

FEEDBACK ON REFLECTIVE ACTIVITY

We have argued that neurotic behaviour can be characterised by mild symptoms of mental illness. The individual is aware that they are behaving in a way that is 'unusual'. This does not sound like Munchausen's syndrome. In our classification of mental illness, Munchausen's syndrome appears to be more of a psychosis, with similarities to schizophrenia. The American functionalist sociologist Talcott Parsons (1967) has popularised the notion of 'the sick role'. Parsons argues that we are likely to accept that someone is sick if they fulfil particular role expectations. Some of these expectations are that the sick person should stop work. They should also seek medical help so that they can get better. We have an expectation in our mind about what this sick person should do, and if the individual does not follow this expectation, we are less likely to accept that they are sick in the conventional meaning of the word (Ingleby 2010).

Someone with Munchausen's syndrome may be perceived as contradicting key aspects of the sick role, such as 'feigning illness' as opposed to being legitimately sick. This is because an individual with Munchausen's syndrome may be viewed as unwilling to get better. The judgement may be made that Munchausen's syndrome represents evidence of deviance as opposed to illness (Ingleby 2010). This reveals, once again, the complexity of classifying mental illnesses.

THE TREATMENT OF MENTAL ILLNESS

REFLECTIVE ACTIVITY 7.5

If you were working as a social worker with someone and they made you aware that they were experiencing feelings of anxiety, an inability to relax, headaches, dizziness and difficulty making decisions, how can our three sociological models help in this situation?

FEEDBACK

A key component of the effective functioning of our society is the health service. We have had a national health service since 1948, and treatment for neuroses and psychoses is available. The symptoms experienced by the person you are working with will, however, be particular to them. This is how interactionism can be helpful. If we become aware of the pressures that exist within capitalist economies and that these pressures can generate mental illnesses, we are applying the principles of conflict theory.

The therapeutic methods available for treating those who have mental illnesses generally fall into one of two categories: psychological or psychiatric (Ingleby 2010). A helpful way of understanding the difference between psychological and psychiatric therapies is that the former therapies do not apply drugs, and the latter therapies are based on the application of drugs (ibid.). The following section of the chapter outlines a number of key therapies that are available to treat mental illnesses.

Psychoanalysis

Psychoanalytical therapy claims that mental disorders arise as a result of the unresolved conflict between the individual components of the personality. This links psychoanalysis to the ideas of the interactionists. It is considered that there are unconscious 'repressed' thoughts influencing the individual's behaviour. The aim of psychoanalysis is to bring these repressed thoughts into the conscious mind so that they can be resolved. The therapeutic process involves techniques such as 'free association' (or talking about whatever comes to mind), 'dream analysis' and 'hypnotherapy'. All of these techniques enable the individual to become aware of conflicts that, in some cases, date back to early childhood. Once the conflicts are brought into awareness, they can then be 'worked through' until the individual's problem is resolved (ibid.).

Behavioural therapies

This way of dealing with mental illness is based on conflict theory. The therapy considers the individual's surroundings and explores how these conditions influence their state of mind. With extreme phobias, it is believed that the phobic person has learned to be afraid of the feared object due to their circumstances. The aim of behavioural therapies is to 'unlearn' this negative association through techniques such as a 'systematic desensitisation'. This therapy works by substituting the learned response of fear for the alternative response of relaxation (ibid.). By teaching the person to relax, the phobic object can then be introduced gradually, until a stage is reached when the individual can face the object without experiencing any fear. The person has then been 'desensitised' to the object in a systematic way.

Cognitive-behavioural therapies

Behavioural techniques such as systematic desensitisation tend to focus on the maladaptive or abnormal behaviour. Less attention is paid to the individual's thinking or reasoning processes. The therapies are less related to interactionism as they examine the environmental factors that are influencing individuals. With cognitive-behavioural therapies, behaviour modification techniques are combined with attempts to identify the inner cognitive functioning of the individual. The behavioural therapies aim to enable the individual to deal with environmental pressures. Conflict theorists are interested in whether these pressures are a result of working conditions. The individual might be taught relaxation techniques in order to cope with symptoms of anxiety such as panic attacks. In addition, the therapist tries to explore the individual and subjective causes of anxiety. Interactionist theorists are interested in these factors. By combining these approaches, the therapist is able to deal with environmental and individual causes of anxious behaviour.

Humanistic counselling

Humanistic counselling is based on what is known as 'the phenomenological approach' (Ingleby 2010). The individual is at the centre of this form of therapy, the goal being to get the individual 'back on course'. This approach is very closely related to interactionism. The therapist is responsible for enabling the individual to explore individual thoughts and emotions in order to resolve feelings of anxiety. It is believed that anxiety is a product of a 'would/should' dilemma. The individual wants to do something but they are not able to act on this wish. The therapist works with the individual in order to resolve this would/should dilemma, and it is argued that the consequence leads to a change in their maladaptive or abnormal behaviour (Ingleby 2010).

Eclectic approaches

The eclectic approach to treating mental illness involves combining techniques. We have seen that the social world can be understood in a profound way if we combine functionalism, interactionism and conflict theory. The aim is to provide a comprehensive 'all round' therapeutic framework, tailored to the individual's specific needs (Ingleby 2010). One particular example of the application of an eclectic approach can be seen with family therapy. The rationale behind this type of therapy rests in the belief that individual problems are often caused or exacerbated by communication or relationship difficulties within the family. In other words, wider environmental factors are considered and, once again, this links to conflict theory. Individual therapy is regarded as being less important because, after each therapeutic session, the individual returns to a disturbed family environment (Ingleby 2010). In family therapy, the whole family meets with one or two therapists, who observe the interactions and relationships within what is known as 'the family system' (Ingleby 2010). In this way, each family member is made aware of how the individual relates to the others and how this interaction is contributing to the family's problems.

Even though it is difficult to categorise mental illnesses, we have seen in this chapter that some forms of mental illness can be treated through psychoanalytic, behavioural, cognitive-behavioural, humanistic and eclectic therapies. We have also seen that an awareness of functionalism, interactionism and conflict theory can help us to understand some of the issues that are associated with mental illnesses. The next section of the chapter reflects on the application of what are referred to as 'physical' therapies for treating mental illness. Physical therapies are characterised by some form of medical intervention, from the administration of drugs through to major surgical procedures.

Psychotherapeutic interventions

From the 1950s onwards, a number of drug therapies became available for the treatment of some forms of mental illness. This development interests functionalist sociologists as it reveals the importance of having a well-developed system of health care. The use of drugs to regulate mental illnesses was regarded as a major breakthrough in psychiatric care in the 1950s (Ingleby 2010). Until then, severely mentally ill individuals were often incarcerated in asylums – literally removed from society. The emergence of psychotherapeutic drugs enabled some forms of mental illness to become less threatening to individuals outside the asylums, so this allowed some mentally ill patients to be discharged from medical institutions. If we apply the ideas of the functionalists, we can argue that this is because of the development of socially regulated health care for the mentally ill. The three main categories of psychotherapeutic drugs that began to be applied through the 1950s were anti-anxiety drugs, anti-psychotic drugs and antidepressants (Ingleby 2010).

Anti-anxiety drugs

These drugs are referred to colloquially as 'tranquillisers'. They work by depressing the nervous system, so they produce feelings of relaxation in order to relieve tension. Although the drugs do appear to alleviate anxiety, they have addictive tendencies and so they are used with caution.

Anti-psychotic drugs

These drugs are most commonly used in the treatment of extreme psychoses, for example schizophrenia. They aim to restore chemical imbalances within the brain. Again, the drugs emerge from a developed medical system, so this interests functionalist sociologists. A problem with this form of drug therapy occurs with the side effects resulting from the drugs. These side effects appear to differ from one person to the next, so this is of interest to interactionist sociologists.

Antidepressants

This group of drugs is used to change the mood of depressed individuals, hence their name. Antidepressants work by restoring chemical imbalances in the brain. These chemical imbalances are believed to influence mood swings. Although the drugs can alleviate some forms of depression, they do not 'cure' the condition. For this reason, the drugs are used in conjunction with some of the therapeutic approaches previously discussed.

Electroconvulsive treatment (ECT)

The reflection from Plath at the beginning of the chapter is about electroconvulsive therapy (or ECT). Strong electric currents are sent through the individual, resulting in massive convulsions. ECT is still used today in cases of severe depression, often when other treatments have failed. The individual is given an anaesthetic and a muscle relaxant to facilitate the treatment. There are side effects, including memory loss, but it is argued that there are also potential benefits associated with ECT, including improvements in 'mood'.

Psychosurgery

Psychosurgery attempts to amend selected areas of the brain in order to alleviate severe psychological and behavioural symptoms. As with ECT, this particular form of treatment has received negative publicity, for example in novels such as *One Flew Over the Cuckoo's Nest*. Functionalist sociologists are interested in considering whether this is an example of dysfunctional medicine. The procedure is controversial. It may lead to the relief of symptoms of mental illness but other cognitive faculties can be adversely affected. More modern techniques and refinements have lessened the risk of the side effects but, like ECT, the procedure tends to be administered when other forms of treatment have not worked.

REFLECTIVE ACTIVITY 7.6

What are the sociological objections to psychosurgery?

FEEDBACK ON REFLECTIVE ACTIVITY

We have noted that functionalists are interested in the medical system within a social group. Ideally, the procedures emerging from this medical system are of benefit to individuals. Psychosurgery, however, appears to inadvertently harm individuals. This is an example of a dysfunctional medical procedure. The universal nature of psychosurgery receives criticism from interactionist sociologists, as they maintain the significance of individual diversity. Conflict theorists are interested in who receives these medical procedures. Are those who protest against capitalist regimes being brought under control through receiving psychosurgery?

So far, we have looked at mental illness and abnormal behaviour, in general. The final section of the chapter considers the sociological implications of a specific mental illness by reflecting on some of the issues surrounding schizophrenia.

THE SOCIOLOGICAL INTEREST IN SCHIZOPHRENIA

In this section of the chapter, schizophrenia is considered as an example of a psychotic mental disorder. The content explores the symptoms of schizophrenia, the possible explanations of its causes and the treatments that are available to help alleviate its effects.

Symptoms of schizophrenia

Schizophrenia is an umbrella term for a group of disorders: there is not one single condition. Generally speaking, schizophrenia is characterised by a severe disorganisation or disruption of the individual's personality, a distorted view of reality and an inability to function effectively in everyday life (Ingleby 2010). Some of the specific symptoms are outlined below.

Disturbances of perception

We can identify some of these disturbances of perception if we reflect on how patients with schizophrenia speak and write. In writing, the words may be combined into small phrases that make initial sense but, when the words are developed into a sentence, they appear to be completely meaningless (Ingleby 2010). For example:

> I am referring to a previous document when I made some remarks that were facts also tested and there is another that concerns me my daughter she has a lobed bottom right ear, her name being Mary Lou. (Atkinson et al. 1987: 618)

These disturbances of thought may also lead to delusions or misinterpretations of reality. The most common delusions are beliefs that external forces are controlling the individual's thoughts and actions (Ingleby 2010).

Disturbances of self-perception

In acute occurrences of schizophrenia, the individual may report an understanding of the world that can seem unusual. Colours can seem brighter and sounds may appear louder. These experiences can, in turn, influence self-perception. The individual may lose their capacity for self-recognition as everything appears to be so different. They might see their hands as being too large or too small and their eyes may be seen as being out of place on their face (Ingleby 2010).

Disturbances of emotion

Schizophrenia can influence the individual's emotional responses. Amusement may be shown towards experiences that most people would find sad or there may be a lack of emotional response altogether.

Withdrawing from reality

During a schizophrenic episode, the individual may withdraw from contact with others and become absorbed in inner thoughts or fantasies. This state of perception can be so intense that the person is unaware of what day of the month it is or even where they are.

An inability to function

The symptoms that may be experienced by the schizophrenic person can influence their ability to function in everyday life. The consequence can be that they might not be able to complete tasks requiring consistent behaviour, for example paid employment. Their interpersonal relationships may suffer as a consequence.

Causes of schizophrenia

Sociologists are interested in the social causes of schizophrenia but it is important to acknowledge that there are other factors beyond the social world that contribute to its development. A range of factors, including heredity, physiological changes in the brain, social circumstances and the environment, appear to influence the development of schizophrenia. The following section of the chapter looks at some of these genetic, physiological and socio-environmental explanations for schizophrenia. If we are to have a holistic understanding of schizophrenia, it is important to take into consideration the broad range of factors that influence its development.

Genetic factors that influence schizophrenia

Gottesman and Shields (1982) identify that the general incidence of schizophrenia within a local population is usually 1 per cent. If, however, a child has parents who have schizophrenia, there is a 46 per cent chance that this individual will become schizophrenic. Gottesman and Shields assert that there is a genetic factor influencing the development of schizophrenia. Further evidence for this is revealed in studies of twins (Ingleby 2010). Gottesman and Shields (1982) reveal that, again, there is a 46 per cent chance of schizophrenia developing in both identical twins, if one twin exhibits schizophrenic symptoms. This appears to confirm the theory that schizophrenia is influenced by genetic factors. We can ask, however, if the twins are genetically identical, why does this chance not increase to 100 per cent?

REFLECTIVE ACTIVITY 7.7

Why do you think that the risk factor for developing schizophrenia in identical twins is not 100 per cent?

FEEDBACK ON REFLECTIVE ACTIVITY

The answer to this question is of interest to sociologists. This is because there are other factors that are important in the emergence of schizophrenia. If there were a clear and absolute genetic link to schizophrenia, then other factors would not need to be taken into consideration. However, the possession of the genetic potential to develop schizophrenia does appear to be influenced by the social factors that also contribute to the development of this medical condition. In the research of Gottesman and Shields (1982), we find that the development of schizophrenia in the children of schizophrenic parents is reduced to 35 per cent if these children are adopted into a non-schizophrenic family. This appears to confirm that there is more to the development of schizophrenia than pure genetic background (Ingleby 2010).

Physiological causes of schizophrenia

If we accept Gottesman and Shields' findings, it is important to study exactly how these genetic factors influence the development of schizophrenia. In order to help us to understand the causes of schizophrenia, natural scientists have studied the genetic factors that produce biochemical imbalances in the brain. It is argued that these biochemical imbalances result in the symptoms that are associated with schizophrenia. One of these influential 'biochemical imbalance' theories is known as the 'dopamine hypothesis' (Ingleby 2010). Saunders and Gejman (2001) popularised this theory by demonstrating that dopamine is a chemical substance that acts as a neurotransmitter. In other words, it carries information around the brain and it is believed to play a vital role in regulating emotions. The dopamine hypothesis is based on accepting that an excess of dopamine within the individual produces symptoms of schizophrenia. This occurs when the nerve cells connect with one another, resulting in the display of schizophrenic behaviour. The evidence for this theory comes from two main sources. First, drugs that reduce the symptoms of schizophrenia work by reducing the levels of dopamine in the brain. This appears to suggest that the behavioural symptoms of schizophrenia are connected to the levels of dopamine in the brain. Second, it has been shown that amphetamine abuse can result in psychotic symptoms in individuals that closely resemble the symptoms of schizophrenia. Amphetamines are known to increase dopamine levels in the brain, so this is a highly significant finding. In addition to these findings, it has been discovered that if amphetamine users are given the same drug therapy that is used in the alleviation of schizophrenia, then this is helpful in relieving the negative effects of amphetamine use. This appears to suggest that if dopamine activity in the brain is increased, for example with amphetamines, we see the occurrence of schizophrenic symptoms (Ingleby 2010). Likewise, if dopamine levels are decreased with anti-psychotic drugs, the symptoms are alleviated. Thus, dopamine levels do seem to play a key role in the aetiology and manifestation of schizophrenia (ibid.). This discovery has emerged from highly sophisticated scientific research. Functionalist sociologists are interested in the social circumstances that can result in the emergence of the highly developed health care systems.

Social theories of schizophrenia

Alongside the hereditary and biochemical influences on the development of schizophrenia, we also need to take into consideration socio-environmental influences. The individual's family environment and the stress that they are experiencing in life appear to be particularly important factors to consider. Family therapy concentrates on analysing the relationships and communication patterns within the family environment. During the 1950s and 1960s, researchers explored the influence of communication and relationship patterns on schizophrenia. The research aimed at identifying how attitudes and behaviour within the family influenced the emergence of schizophrenia. Three of these factors appear to be particularly important.

Double-bind communication

This example of communication was popularised by Gregory Bateson (1972). The child receives contradictory messages of communication from its parents. The child may be 'loved and praised' and then subsequently not loved alongside being criticised. These forms of communication are expressed by the parents in verbal and non-verbal ways. The parents do not necessarily realise that they are communicating like this but the child receives a series of mixed messages. A way of dealing with this situation is for the child to withdraw into their own world, away from everyone else. In this situation, family therapy may help to address these difficulties of communication and the harmful effects on the child.

Pseudomutuality

This term refers to relationships within the family environment that are rarely favourable or 'mutual'. It can be argued that all of us can experience a degree of ambivalence or negativity towards family members at some time, whether this is annoyance or jealousy or anger (Ingleby 2010). It can also be argued that it is important to resolve this ambivalence if the relationships in the family are to remain positive. The difficulty appears to arise when this ambivalence is not addressed, and may result in what Wynne et al. (1977) refer to as 'pseudomutuality', or 'false mutuality'. It can appear that all is fine within the family when this is not really the case, and this, again, produces mixed messages. It is thought that children are especially sensitive to this situation of pretence, and as with the occurrence of 'double-bind communication', it is argued that this confusing family background may lead to the behavioural symptoms of schizophrenia. Conflict theorists are interested in the economic pressures that may lead to a sense of false mutuality. Families with so much material wealth may not need to rely on each other. This can exacerbate feelings of false mutuality and this may, in turn, result in the emergence of symptoms of schizophrenia.

Marital schism and skew

'Marital schism' occurs when the parents' relationship is poor but they stay together 'for the sake of the children'. What then might happen is a situation where the children are treated with kindness by their parents but they also become aware of the tense relationship that exists between their parents. With 'marital skew', we see the emergence of a family environment in which one parent denies the negative qualities of his or her partner. These qualities are patently obvious to the child, but they are being ignored. The argument runs, once again, that these mixed messages are conducive to producing schizophrenic behaviour (Ingleby 2010). The work of Albert Bandura (1977) can be applied to identify how marital schism and marital skew produce schizophrenic behaviour in family members. Bandura writes about 'social learning theory'. The key message from this theory is the realisation that imitation depends upon making an emotional connection with others. If this emotional connection is lost, then there is less possibility of imitation. Both marital schism and marital skew are likely to produce emotional tensions between parents and children. The children may define themselves in ways that are opposite to how their parents are behaving, and this may, in turn, produce behaviours that appear to be 'schizophrenic'. As opposed to having a household that is based on mutual respect and love, there is a household of tension and perceived schizophrenic behavioural traits.

REFLECTIVE ACTIVITY 7.8

A social worker who visited a local primary school noted that, during 'play time', there was an unusual 'wall of silence'. This was because all the children were playing in isolation on their mobile electronic devices. How does this social environment connect to what we have been discussing in the chapter?

FEEDBACK ON REFLECTIVE ACTIVITY

This is an interesting example of how social circumstances may influence the development of symptoms of schizophrenia. In this case, there is an absence of 'mutuality'. The children do not depend on each other for companionship: they have their mobile devices and they are able to play on these devices in isolation. As a consequence of 'isolating technology' they may not develop the same social skills that previous groups of children developed. A conflict theorist will be interested in a situation where the material wealth of a social group results in gadgets that produce isolated behaviour. In this instance, technology may be producing social conditions that lead to the emergence of schizophrenia.

You may have experienced some of these circumstances and you may agree that technology is not always good for the development of children. The complexity of schizophrenia is also revealed in this example. Why don't we all exhibit schizophrenic symptoms as a consequence of isolating technology? It can be argued that schizophrenia appears to be influenced by a range of complex factors: some of these factors are genetic and physiological, and other factors are social and environmental. This complex set of factors influencing the emergence of schizophrenia may result in individuals who are born with a genetic predisposition towards schizophrenia, but the condition needs to be 'triggered' later in life either by a specific stressful event, such as bereavement, or by a series of more general stressful circumstances, such as dysfunctional family communication (Ingleby 2010). This explanation of the way in which the components of schizophrenia interact together is referred to as the 'diathesis-stress model' of mental illness. This theory was initially popularised by Thomas Holmes and Richard Rahe (1967). The theory is based on studying the relationship that exists between stressful life events and the onset of schizophrenia in adults. Holmes and Rahe's 'Social Readjustment Rating Scale' provides an estimate of an individual's stress level on the basis of assessing the individual's vulnerability to a number of stressful events which they are experiencing over a period of time (six months to one year). It is argued that people with schizophrenia often report experiencing more of these stressful events than non-schizophrenic individuals. This appears to support the argument that there is a relationship between stress and the development of schizophrenia.

It can also be argued that perhaps those who experience the symptoms of schizophrenia are more likely to perceive life to be more stressful than 'normal' individuals. Nonetheless, Holmes and Rahe's (ibid.) work is important in that it reveals that stress in social life is a factor influencing symptoms of schizophrenia.

This chapter has revealed that the causes of schizophrenia are complex, and that a range of factors need to be considered. These factors are genetic and they also link to family environment and personal levels of stress. Additional factors, such as sex, socio-economic status, environment, for example urban or rural, race and social support are also identified as being influential in the development of this disorder (Ingleby 2010).

Treating schizophrenia

Ideally, the treatment of schizophrenia employs a combination of physical and psychological therapies. Anti-psychotic drugs should be used in conjunction with individual and/or family therapy. This ideally leads to the treatment of the immediate situation, the symptoms, and the underlying problems that are leading to the development of schizophrenia. The book reveals the reality that we do not live in an ideal world. This eclectic approach may be ideal, but it can be difficult to realise because of resources and social circumstances. This is again of interest to our sociological models. Individual psychotherapy is not always possible and anti-psychotic drugs may not be available because of socio-economic factors. The factors influencing the emergence of schizophrenia and its treatment appear to depend on a complex range of circumstances. The emergence of a society's medical system, the individual development of schizophrenia and the economic factors influencing schizophrenia will interest functionalist, interactionist and conflict theorists.

CONCLUSION

This chapter began by identifying what our three groups of sociologists would find interesting about mental illness. We have seen that functionalist sociologists look at the wider social factors that influence the perception of health and well-being.

Particular societies understand mental illnesses in particular ways. We have seen that, in this society, there has been a change in the perception of mental illness, and the religious interpretation of mental illness is now influenced by medical under-standings of the world. The complex medical system of the UK, with its network of scientific research into mental illness, interests functionalist sociologists. In contrast, the individual responses to mental illnesses are of interest to interactionist sociolo-gists, whereas conflict theorists draw attention to the economic conditions that are influencing mental health and well-being. The chapter has also reflected on a case study of schizophrenia. We have considered some of the range of genetic, physiolog-ical and socio-economic factors influencing the emergence of schizophrenia in individuals. It can be argued that this eclectic approach may be the best way to understand this complex medical condition and its consequences.

CHAPTER 8

OLDER PEOPLE, SOCIOLOGY AND SOCIAL WORK

INTRODUCTION

They umm-ed and they aah-ed and they stared towards the ceiling, chewing pencils to destruction over 16 across. It was hell out there in the Great Western Suite of the Paddington Hilton in London yesterday as the cream of *The Telegraph* crossword enthusiasts, plucked from breakfast tables, garden recliners and commuter trains across the land, joined battle in the same room.

The silence was deafening, broken only by the hum of the air conditioning and the throb of brains struggling over 'Inconsistent statement in Pope's document (4)' and 'Bacon could be comparatively audacious (6)'. Finally, 30 minutes and 24 seconds into the competition, a hand shot up, waving in the air. It belonged to Brian Murgatroyd, aged 66, a retired tax inspector from High Wycombe, Herts, and when his answers were checked, they were all correct. (Ingleby, 2010 p92)

In our culture, we might not assume automatically that the winner of a test for mental agility would be an older person. The images of older people in this country are not necessarily positive. There appears to be a perception that older people are a potential problem: a drain on resources. The implication can be that retirement and old age are not welcome. This chapter considers the contribution that sociology can make to social work when we are working with older people, and explores the social construction of old age. The content outlines how the physical changes that are associated with old age should be placed into context. They only become significant when there is an associated social interpretation of old age. The content begins by outlining functionalist, interactionist and conflict theory interest in old age, and a discussion about the social implications of ageing follows. We will reflect on definitions of old age and explore theories that account for the ageing process. Throughout the chapter, we will focus on explaining how theories allied to sociology can help your professional practice when you are working with older people.

FUNCTIONALIST INTEREST IN OLD AGE

We have seen in this book that functionalists look at the bigger picture. In exemplifying this point, they are more interested in art galleries in their entirety as opposed to focusing on individual paintings in the gallery. Functionalist sociologists are interested in the wider interpretations of old age that exist within a society and how these interpretations differ according to social contexts. In anthropological accounts of other societies, we see differences in the interpretation of social groups. First Nation Americans are known to show respect to older people, and the wisdom of older people appears to be appreciated. In other cultural contexts, this respect is not necessarily shown to older people. In the UK, it is predicted that, by 2020, the demographic profile of the country will be characterised by the presence of more people who are over 60 years of age than those who are under this age. The presence of older people in large numbers appears to exaggerate the social interpretation of ageing. In societies such as the UK's, older people may be shown less respect than in other societies. Old age is experienced in all cultures; however, the social interpretation that is given to ageing differs across cultural contexts. Functionalists are also interested in how societies respond to meet the needs of older people. In the UK, there are a series of social reforms that have been introduced to help older people, including the provision of a state pension. This state pension has emerged due to the social circumstances in our country. Particular governments have identified the importance of protecting older people. Functionalist sociologists are interested in how these socio-political factors influence the experience of old age. The laws that exist to protect older people in our society are not just produced by individuals – they represent social consensus. These laws are generated in this country by a law-making body residing within the government. The effectiveness of the law with respect to its influence on the characteristics of the social world is of interest to functionalist sociologists. The practice of social workers is, in turn, influenced by these social processes. As a social worker, your work with older people has been influenced in a profound way by the nature of the law-making processes of our society. Although attempts have been made to protect older people under law, there are always exceptions to the rule and this interests functionalist sociologists. The presence of exceptions to the law reveals the importance of having qualified social workers who are able to work effectively with older people who may be vulnerable.

INTERACTIONIST INTEREST IN OLDER PEOPLE

We have seen that interactionists trace their work back to the philosophy of Kant. The interactionist project is concerned with exploring individual interpretations of the social world, therefore interactionist sociologists are concerned with individual experiences of old age. Emphasis is placed on how these individual experiences are generated and the consequences that these experiences have for individual social workers working with older people. The advantage of this approach to sociology rests in its ability to appreciate the general exceptions to any given rule. In the previous section, we gave a general account of old age and argued that, whereas some societies respect older people, other societies are less welcoming of old age. We have a welfare state and a generous state pension in this country, but this does not necessarily mean that older people will be content in UK society. Although older people share common factors, the experience of old age varies across individuals. There are a common set of health challenges that may impact upon older people, but these health problems are experienced in unique ways. Interactionism helps social workers to understand the particular characteristics of older people. If we consider that older people are unique and that they understand their world in a unique way, we are more likely to adopt a client-centred approach. As opposed to categorising groups of individuals, we see our purpose as meeting the needs of a diverse range of clients. This philosophy of social work enables us to respect the rights of individuals. There are many older people who experience debilitating illnesses, yet there are also many older people who do not experience these illnesses. These individuals may have a perfectly normal life and it is only through recognising this individual approach that we are able to work effectively with older people. The benefit of interactionism to working with older people is seen in the opening quotation of this chapter. We are able to appreciate the exceptions to the rule as opposed to basing our professional practice on sets of general assumptions.

CONFLICT THEORY AND OLDER PEOPLE

Conflict theorists are interested in economic forces and the way in which material conditions influence groups of individuals within social groups. Older people are typically viewed as being a vulnerable social group. Physical decline occurs with old age and this can result in vulnerability. Conflict theorists are interested in how well looked after or otherwise our older population is. The material circumstances of previous times in this country have meant that older people may not have had a positive experience of old age. We have seen in Victorian Britain that there was no national health service, and individuals were reliant on informal services provided by family and friends. This situation resulted from an economy that is referred to as 'laissez-faire': the governments of the time literally let matters run their course. Little was done in society, and the prevailing philosophy was one of not intervening within the social world. Conflict theorists are interested in the consequences of this approach for sections of society. We can argue that this economic approach was not good for older people – there were no systematic attempts being made to intervene so that the lives of older people would be made better. It was believed that this laissez-faire approach was better for the economy. Low taxation allows the rich to get richer as they are able to speculate and potentially accumulate even more wealth. Conflict theorists draw attention to the contradictions that are associated with laissez-faire economies: there is a fraction of very wealthy individuals and a majority who live in poverty. In Victorian England, we witnessed urban cities like London emerging, and these cities were characterised by a demographic structure of few older people and many children. Victorian families were typically very large because so many children died, and with a large family of many children there was a chance that at least some of the children might survive. As the economic relations in the UK changed, so we see the emergence of a welfare state. Socialism became accepted as attempts were made to make society more equal, and this, in turn, led to the social reforms that were at the centre of the welfare state. In the UK, today, we see older people being looked after with a state pension and the National Health Service, and these reforms make it easier for older people to adjust to the experience of old age. It is generally considered that a purpose of the state is to help and support older people. In the UK, the provision of state services has improved over time. The benefit of conflict theory to social workers rests in its ability to enhance our awareness of the potential impact of economic circumstances on the lives of older people.

WHAT IS OLD AGE?

We can say that another phrase for old age is 'the process of ageing'. There is, however, a vague quality to this phrase. In framing the content of the chapter, it is worth reflecting on what we consider constitutes 'old age'.

REFLECTIVE ACTIVITY 8.1

What is 'old age'?

FEEDBACK ON REFLECTIVE ACTIVITY

The challenge in defining 'old age' rests in the variable interpretations of who is old. A man who is 50 years old may regard himself as being 'old' but he is still expected to go

(Continued)

(Continued)

to work and he is not likely to retire in the UK until he is aged at least 65 years. There are subjective factors influencing old age as well as legal understandings of who is an older person. If you are not retired from work and you are not receiving a pension, you may consider yourself to be 'young'. Age appears to vary from place to place, across time and space. In countries with emerging populations (for example, Malaysia), the perception of old age differs from that in the UK. The demography of Malaysia sees a young population who are economically active as opposed to the ageing population we witness in nations like the UK. If we were able to travel back in time in this country, we would see a very different demographic profile. In Victorian Britain, conditions in the towns and cities were not conducive to supporting large numbers of older people. We may be a very different nation to Malaysia, but our population structure has shared similar characteristics.

The same issue arises if we try to define who is 'young'. All of these categories are social constructions. This interests our sociological theorists. We can argue that certain categories of age have been socially invented. The teenage culture we witness in the UK today was not always present – it is a social invention that is influenced by social structures, individual perceptions and economic forces. The relative nature of defining age becomes a topic of interest in itself.

THEORIES EXPLAINING THE AGEING PROCESS THAT ARE USEFUL TO SOCIOLOGY AND SOCIAL WORK

There are a number of theories that explain the processes involved in physical ageing, and these theories are useful for sociologists and social workers. This section of the chapter reflects on three of these theories. Although the chapter is not about the detailed biological changes that we experience as we age, it is important to acknowledge the connection that exists between an individual's physical ageing and their social circumstances. This, in turn, influences social perceptions of ageing.

Wear and tear theory

Klatz and Goldman (1997) emphasise the importance of 'wear and tear' theory. An analogy is made between the human body and a machine. The assumption is made that, just as machines such as cars 'wear out', so similar processes are experienced by human beings. Time becomes the critical factor in wear and tear theory. Over time, the human body is regarded as becoming vulnerable to the physical factors that can lead to physical decline and death. This 'assumption' equates time with physical vulnerability.

REFLECTIVE ACTIVITY 8.2

What is problematic in wear and tear theory?

FEEDBACK ON REFLECTIVE ACTIVITY

A major problem with this theory is the assumption that human beings deteriorate over time. Human development is not a continuum and this is a false way of looking at growth and development. There are exceptions to what is anticipated due to social and genetic variables. For example, someone may be relatively unfit and then exercise from the age of 40 years so that they experience physical improvements between the ages of 40 to 50 years. We can argue that wear and tear theory is too simplistic and too general in claiming that as people get older, their bodies 'wear out' (Ingleby 2010). We need a theory that has applicability as opposed to basing our understanding of ageing on superficial levels of explanation.

Cellular theory

James (1995) defines 'cellular' theory as the investigation of how disease results from micro-organisms that exist within the cells of the body. The theory explores how errors in cell division occurring throughout life contribute to the degenerative conditions we experience in later years (ibid.). To exemplify this point, an 'error' during the process of cell division may result in two faulty cells, which can, in turn, divide to form four faulty cells, dividing again to produce eight faulty cells and so on. Over the course of time, these faulty cells will begin to impair the function of the part of the body in which they are to be found (Ingleby 2010). A further area of interest in cellular theory is the impact that toxic substances have on the human body. Cellular theory provides explanations of ageing that are based on 'accumulation theories' (ibid.). These theories explore the changes in the human body that influence the ability to get rid of metabolic waste. Cellular theory also explores the impact of what are known as 'collagens': some substances such as 'lipofuscin' begin to build up in the body with advancing age, and, after many years of accumulation, this substance begins to form areas of darker pigmentation on the skin. These collagen fibres are found in the body, particularly in muscles, joints and bones. With increased age, these fibrous proteins become thicker, less elastic and less soluble (ibid.). Eventually, they may replace existing tissues to produce visible signs of ageing, for example wrinkling of the skin, sagging muscles and slower healing of wounds.

Immunity theory

Metchnikoff (2000) has popularised 'immunity' theory. The theory explains ageing by focusing on the physiological changes that are associated with the ageing process, and suggests that changes within the body's immune system produce physical degeneration (Ingleby 2010). With age, the immune system is less efficient and cells that are harmful to the body are able to cause damage to the body. This, in turn, results in physical degeneration. There are variations to immunity theory: one strand of the theory argues that the immune system is not able to recognise deviations or faults in molecular structure and cell characteristics. Cells that have undergone mutation and would normally have been destroyed by the immune system are no longer recognised. They are then allowed by the body to grow and develop in ways that are harmful to health. A second strand of immunity theory explores why the body is not able to produce the antibodies that are needed to destroy harmful cells. A third strand explores how ageing is linked to the development of antibodies within the body that destroy cells that are normal and healthy. This results in the auto-immune antibodies working in a harmful way (ibid.).

REFLECTIVE ACTIVITY 8.3

How can cellular theory and immunity theory inform sociology and social work?

FEEDBACK ON REFLECTIVE ACTIVITY

Both of these theories draw attention to the physical processes associated with biological maturation. Any social worker who is going to work with older people needs to become aware of the consequences of old age for older people. The theories also reveal that the importance attached to these physical processes of ageing vary according to social context. In the UK, there are a relative high number of older people. The functioning of our society involves considering the needs of older people. It is, however, important to acknowledge the interactionist emphasis that is placed on individual responses to old age. Physiological changes do not necessarily produce the same physical effects and problems in all older people. When it is also shown that physical ageing links to economic factors (for example, the consequences of an industrial revolution), this also strengthens the argument that understandings of age depend on social circumstances.

REFLECTIVE ACTIVITY 8.4

Why do you think that there is interest in cellular and immunity theories in the UK?

FEEDBACK ON REFLECTIVE ACTIVITY

We have seen that the functionalist sociologist Talcott Parsons explores the nature of being 'sick' within social groups (1967). Parsons' work draws attention to the social factors that influence perceptions of health in social groups. In the UK, we are influenced by a medical model of health that assumes that 'cure A' can be administered to 'condition B' following diagnosis from a medical practitioner. This accounts for the importance of medical interest in the ageing process. Our sociological theorists are interested in how and why particular theories become influential in social groups. In conflict theory, we see the concept of hegemony being explored: an elite group begins to dominate society and understandings of the social world are shaped by their concerns. This has happened in the UK because medical understandings of old age dominate our perception of the processes of ageing.

In other cultures, the challenges that are associated with ageing may be explained in religious ways. They may be interpreted as being consequences of divine powers. In UK society, the prevailing social power has generated a medical understanding of the world and this is accepted in general as an explanation of the ageing process.

EXTERNAL SIGNS OF AGEING

A number of physical signs of ageing are shared across social groups. These factors include the wrinkling of the skin, tiredness, slower movement and weakening of the bones. Pain in the joints can become more common, and posture may become stooped. The hair may turn grey or white or be lost. All of these signs of physical ageing are shared across cultures.

It is, however, important to remember that the emphasis placed on these physical signs of ageing depends on social factors and perceptions can be stereotypical. It is not the case that older people are always experiencing sickness and poor health, but this can be a perception of the ageing process in our society. Although there are older people who need care and assistance, there are also other older people who lead completely independent lives. So, old age is not necessarily synonymous with being in a state of poor health. Starr and Weiner (1981) confirm this point in their study of the health status of a sample of people aged between 60 and 90 years. The key finding in this study reveals that a number of significant factors influence the social construction of old age. Over 70 per cent of the research participants in this study described their health as 'excellent' or 'good', with 25 per cent describing their health as 'fair' and 3 per cent viewing their health as being 'poor'. This reveals the strength of the interactionist argument that we need to consider the perceptions of individuals if we are to understand the social world.

This is not to say that there are no discernible physical and mental changes associated with old age. We have already made reference to the physical changes in older people that result from the ageing process. As we have argued, however, it is the social interpretation of these physical changes that appears to be particularly important to the work of social workers. The next section of the chapter reflects on the sociological consequences of these examples of physical ageing.

Skin

Holliday (1995) outlines how the ageing process leads to wrinkling of the skin. With age, there is a loss of subcutaneous fat tissue and skin elasticity. This reduces the life of skin cells in those who are aged 70 years and above to 46 days, compared with about 100 days for a 30-year-old (idid.). Alongside this change, the cells themselves are replaced more slowly and the skin loses its ability to retain fluids so it can appear dry and lacking flexibility. Accompanying the physiological changes that are associated with the skin is the gradual inability to regulate body temperature. This can pose challenges for the body's immunity system and make individuals more vulnerable to poor health. The social consequences of this form of ageing appear to vary according to social groups. In UK society, there are all sorts of creams and lotions that add moisture to the skin, the implication being that there is a loss of beauty as the skin ages. Although this is a common perception in the UK, the other potential health consequences associated with the skin ageing may not be as widely understood. This reveals that there are perceptions of reality being influenced by social factors. The association of ageing skin with a loss of beauty tends to be emphasised to the detriment of other potential consequences. Sociologists are interested in how and why this social construction occurs.

Hair

Johnson (2005) reflects on the physical and psychological consequences of the ageing process. In UK society, 'good hair', like 'good skin', is regarded as being a desirable physical attribute. With advancing age, human hair can become grey and lose its lustre. Many individuals experience a thinning of the hair and a high proportion of men eventually become bald. Hair loss on the arms and legs may also occur with age. In women, a change in the androgen/oestrogen hormonal ratio can lead to the production of facial hair on the upper lip and chin. These physical changes are given a negative interpretation in general in UK society. In our consumer culture, a message is provided that consumer power is equated with appearance. Good skin and good hair appear as favourable signs that the individual will be able to obtain the rest of the material trappings that equate with commercial power, therefore older people who do not have good hair or good skin may be disadvantaged. Stereotyping, prejudice and discrimination may also result from judgements that are based on appearances.

Teeth

With age, many older people are faced with the prospect of a permanent loss of teeth. Steele et al. (1998) calculate that, by the age of 75 years, the average person has lost all but 15 of their teeth. Dentures become the norm for most people in this situation. In the UK, an emphasis is placed on having 'good teeth', in a similar way to the importance of good hair and good skin. Physical beauty, youth, vitality and consumer power are associated with a 'perfect smile'. Older people are often perceived as being the antithesis to this positive image. This social construction, once again, produces risks of stereotyping, prejudice and discrimination for older people.

Posture

Lord et al. (2001) draw attention to the link between age and posture. Older people, in general, experience shrinkage of discs in the spinal column, resulting in a loss of physical stature. Losing collagen between the spinal vertebrae can also cause the spine to bend. This can make older people 'stoop' and gives an impression of loss of height. In UK society, there can be an assumption that a loss of physical strength in old age equates to slowness of mind. This is a social construction. The beginning of the chapter reveals that older people do not necessarily experience mental decline.

REFLECTIVE ACTIVITY 8.5

How can our three sociological theories explain the mental pressures that are placed on older people?

FEEDBACK ON REFLECTIVE ACTIVITY

Functionalists are interested in the wider social factors influencing social groups and the social construction of old age in societies can be interpreted in helpful ways within this perspective. In contrast, interactionists are interested in the individual exceptions to the general social rules. The individual at the beginning of the chapter, who wins the mental agility test, is an older person and, as such, he may be regarded as being an exception to the rule because our society does not in general promote the message that older people are mentally agile. Interactionists argue that the positive examples of old age demonstrated by these exceptions to the rule need to be emphasised. This holds the capacity to change perceptions of old age. Conflict theorists are interested in the consequences of the economy on older people, and it is argued that economic pressures on older people are likely to produce negative effects for their state of mind. The argument runs that a change in economy will produce a change in the older person's state of mind.

MENTAL HEALTH IN OLDER PEOPLE AND SOCIAL WORK

There is a link between physical and mental health. It may be assumed that older people are more likely to be physically frail. This expectation can have social consequences for older people who may be more prone to mental illnesses as a result of this expectation.

Depression

Depression in older people may be a consequence of chronic illnesses, but it may also result from the social expectation that older people are not mentally robust. There can be what Ingleby (2010) refers to as a sense of 'social redundancy'. Biebel and Koenig (2004) describe different forms of depression: there is transient (or 'normal') depression which can take the form of general feelings of sadness that many people experience with bereavement; there is also the experience of prolonged (or 'pathological') depression. This is a much more pervasive and complex state of mind.

REFLECTIVE ACTIVITY 8.6

What is 'depression'?

FEEDBACK ON REFLECTIVE ACTIVITY

The following feelings are all symptoms of depression: unhappiness, tiredness, guilt, hopelessness, helplessness, and apathy. The social significance that is given to depression is important. Most of us, from time to time, experience the emotions that are listed above, but not everyone is diagnosed with depression. There are social factors that influence understandings of depression. In UK society, particular groups are associated with depression, especially those who are regarded as having feelings of low self-esteem. Older people appear to fit into this category. Depression can be associated with older people due to these social factors, and this should be taken into consideration by social workers when they are working with older people.

The social importance of depression

It can be argued that pathological depression can develop as a response to chronic illness or to the general ageing process. Acceptance of becoming older appears to be especially important if depression is to be avoided, as denial of the ageing process appears to be linked to feelings of depression. We can summarise depression in older people in two ways. There is evidence of a depressive mood and a tendency to become helpless: this can result in negativity, limited attention and memory loss (Ingleby 2010). There is also a tendency to focus on debilitating physical complaints so that the individual does less and less activities. We can argue that social factors are important in the development of depression, as the general perception of older people in society may influence the state of mind of an older person. A complexity associated with depression is that it tends to 'feed' on itself (ibid.). Once an older person is diagnosed as depressed, they are likely to accept that this is a fundamental part of their personality. People who are not depressed are less likely to accept their circumstances – they are more likely to look for ways out of their challenging circumstances. Those who are not suffering from depression are more likely to ask for advice so that they can take specific action in order to deal with the situation (ibid.). Depressed people are less likely to demonstrate such rational behaviour. They are, in turn, more likely to exhibit addictive behaviours (for example, addiction to drugs/alcohol) that can exacerbate their challenging circumstances.

The complexity of old age

This chapter has outlined that ageing processes involve external and internal changes to the body. The changes that are associated with old age may lead to the development of various physical, chronic health conditions. It is, however, important that we do not assume that this is always the case. Although chronic illnesses can be a contributory factor in the development of depression, it is not necessarily true that the majority of older people are affected by depression. It is especially important for social workers to be aware that some older people should be left alone to lead as healthy a life as possible. Older people do not necessarily wish to have 'company': they are not necessarily experiencing feelings of loneliness. Indeed, the negative media portrayal of social work can result in a complex situation, where the intervention of social workers is regarded as something that is completely undesirable. The subsequent psychological consequences of this state of mind may lead to anger and violence being directed towards social workers from the older people they are working with.

RESEARCH ACTIVITY

Using online resources, identify whether or not depression is becoming more of a problem for older people in the UK.

The prevalence of mental illness among older people in the UK

In the UK, mental illnesses such as depression do appear to have become a significant issue for older people over time. If we go back to the year 2000, one in six adults in the UK had a neurotic disorder (such as anxiety or depression), while one in seven had considered suicide at some point in their lives. Although the rates of psychiatric disorders were similar in the UK from 1993 to 2000, the proportion of people receiving medical treatment for these disorders increased. In 2000, 24 per cent of these people received treatment compared with 14 per cent in 1993 (Ingleby 2010). This reveals that depression has become an increasing problem in the UK.

Dementia

Cheston and Bender (2003) reflect on the perception of dementia in the UK. Dementia is described as the deterioration of the functioning of the mind. Senile dementia and Alzheimer's disease tend to be associated with older people. Dementia causes changes in thinking patterns as the brain is affected by 'wear and tear'. The consequences result in confusion, paranoia and forgetfulness. Depression, anxiety, inability to concentrate and denial may be the first signs of the disease (Ingleby 2010), and memory loss is a major symptom. From appearing to be 'absent-minded', Alzheimer's disease develops into a debilitating state of mind, where the person is unable to remember their own name. This can lead to a life of chaos and confusion.

In Western cultures, there has been an assumption that Alzheimer's disease is a consequence of senility (Ingleby 2010), and it has been presumed that everyone will develop this condition over time. Functionalist, interactionist and conflict theorists explore the consequences of assumptions like this. Functionalists are interested in the changing social circumstances that influence the development of Alzheimer's disease. Conflict theorists will propose that a link exists between changing economic circumstances and the development of Alzheimer's, and the condition will be regarded as a consequence of capitalism. The aetiology of Alzheimer's disease is more likely to be identified as economic circumstances change and a socialist national health service emerges. Interactionists would highlight the exceptions to the rule – that is, not all older people have Alzheimer's disease. Grey-Davidson (1999) argues that it is important to reflect on the facts that are known about Alzheimer's disease as opposed to simply assuming that all older people are likely to develop this condition. There are a number of possible causes of Alzheimer's disease (ibid.). The condition may result from an imbalance of neurochemicals in the brain. The enzyme choline acetyltransferase is important in the human brain as it regulates the production of acetylcholine. This neurotransmitter influences the functioning of the brain. Irregularities in the presence of this enzyme results in the development of Alzheimer's disease. The accumulation of toxins such as aluminium in the brain is another factor in the emergence of the condition. Genetic and viral factors are also considered to be significant.

The assumption that all older people are predisposed to the development of Alzheimer's disease should be challenged. The mind does not necessarily deteriorate with age. Older people experience a range of social circumstances, and this can actually enrich the mind and produce wisdom. Older people may be referred to with phrases like: 'Who would have thought so?' and 'Can you believe it?' It is important to remember that Alzheimer's disease is not inevitable and that the association of older people with the development of Alzheimer's disease is yet another negative stereotype that is attached to older people.

REFLECTIVE ACTIVITY 8.7

What are the challenges for social workers who are working with older people with Alzheimer's disease, and how can sociology help?

FEEDBACK ON REFLECTIVE ACTIVITY

The personal nature of social work is based on working at relationships. Over time, and with experience, you become a trusted professional as you work with others. Alzheimer's disease can challenge all of this good practice. You are no longer remembered and all the hard work that you have done is lost as your name is not even recalled. Functionalist sociologists highlight what is dysfunctional for societies. Alzheimer's disease threatens the functioning of the social order. It is important for social workers to appreciate the benefits of medical research for those we are working with. In the UK, a strong national health service should be a priority if our work with older people is to be successful.

INTELLECT AND OLDER PEOPLE

There can be a perception that older people are forgetful, that they are muddled in their thoughts and that they are repetitive. These perceptions of older people are social constructions. The application of sociology can help to reveal the myths of old age. These myths can be the basis of stereotypes about old age. Horn and Donaldson (1976, 1977) argue against the assumption that old age equates with losing intellectual faculties. Schaie (1996) reveals that the relationship between the intellect and age is more complicated than we might assume. Bernard et al. (2000, p94) argue that old age does not necessarily equate with a reduction in cognitive ability. Interactionists draw attention to the importance of individuals with respect to their capacity to influence social groups. In our Western culture, the work of the cognitive psychologists Piaget and Vygotsky has had a huge influence on our perception of the functioning of the human mind. Piaget (1962) and Vygotsky (1978) are particularly interested in the development of the child's mind. The indirect consequence of this emphasis has been an assumption that the mind develops in childhood and stagnates in adulthood. This social construction reinforces the assumption that older adults do not have the capacity for cognitive growth and development.

REFLECTIVE ACTIVITY 8.8

Is it true that the mind declines with age?

FEEDBACK ON REFLECTIVE ACTIVITY

Horn and Donaldson (1976, 1977) play a key role in drawing attention to the negative stereotypical attitudes that can be expressed towards older people. Although some aspects of memory, reasoning ability and mental attention span do worsen as a person becomes older, there are aspects of intellect that become better with age. Some older people can witness improvements with their verbal/conceptual ability as they age, and some people get better at maths as they get older. The importance of raised social awareness also appears to increase as the person ages. It is argued that the critical influence in this improvement of cognitive ability is the memory (Ingleby 2010). The perception of old age equating to 'impaired intellect' appears to be nothing other than a social construction.

CASE STUDY

Michael is a retired accountant. He worries about getting older because he thinks that old age equates with a loss of cognitive ability. This is the message of the media and the view of others he knows. He reflects on his younger days and remembers how efficient he was as an accountant between the ages of 50 to 55 years. Michael reflects that those days were his best professional days! He knew everything there was to know about being an accountant and he had all his weekly work finished by lunch time on Fridays. He reflects on those times as being the best of times! If only there was someone he could talk to so that he could be reassured that he was not losing his mental faculties. Perhaps a doctor? Perhaps a social worker who realised that perceptions of old age in our culture are often based on negative social assumptions? Such reassurance would certainly help Michael's peace of mind.

OLDER AGE AND INTELLECTUAL ABILITY

If we apply the work of Horn and Donaldson (1976, 1977) to working with older people, we can contradict the stereotypical notion that old age results in a reduction in intellectual capacity. If verbal/conceptual/mathematical ability and social awareness improves with age, we can argue that older people have many useful cognitive skills. The traditional First Nation perception of older people as wise and needing to be listened to occurs in a particular social context. This more acceptable social context, where older people are valued, appears to be the sort of message that older people should be receiving. It is important to remember that once we become 65 years of age, we do not necessarily experience a loss of intellectual ability.

MEMORY AND AGEING

It is also important to consider the social meaning that is attached to the human memory when we are working with older people. In our culture, there can be a stereotypical assumption that the memory deteriorates with age, but this is not necessarily the case. It is important to reflect on the complexity of the human memory (Ingleby 2010). There are three types of memory: sensory memories, short-term memories and long-term memories. The next section of the chapter reflects on the social importance that is placed on each of these forms of the memory.

Sensory memory

Sensory memory refers to the sensory stimuli we receive (Ingleby 2010), in the form of visual images, sounds and smells. These forms of sensory stimuli produce reactions in us that we remember.

Short-term memory

Short-term memory refers to the individual's immediate attention span. Sprenger (1999, p48) argues that this type of memory has a limited duration and lasts for no more than 30–60 seconds. Maintaining information in the short-term memory is achieved through a process that is referred to as 'rehearsal' (Ingleby 2010). If we are to remember a telephone number, we have to practice memorising the number so that it stays within the short-term memory. A typical strategy involves reciting the number so that we remember it. In an early study in this area in the 1870s, Hermann Ebbinghaus found that he was able to memorise up to seven items in any one attempt, but if he tried to increase this number then it took much longer to memorise this additional information (Ingleby 2010). This work by Ebbinghaus was developed by George Miller in 1956 and resulted in the suggestion that a typical short-term memory can remember between five and nine items. This is known as 'the magic number seven, plus or minus two' (Miller 1956). The work is useful because it draws attention to a cognitive process that is known as 'chunking'. We group information together so that it is memorised in smaller, more manageable chunks. This is then stored within the short-term memory.

REFLECTIVE ACTIVITY 8.9

What contributions can sociology make to help our understanding of memory and older people?

FEEDBACK ON REFLECTIVE ACTIVITY

Our three schools of sociology discuss the impact of social forces on individuals. We have also seen in this book how interactionists emphasise the importance of individuals engaging with social structures, so that new forms of social life are created. So many aspects of the social world appear to be social constructions. The exciting contribution that is made of sociology to this area rests in the realisation that the perception that older people do not have good memories is not necessarily true. If anything, older people might have more profound memories because of their experiences. Older people do not have 'weak memories'. This is a social construction, a perception that is perpetuated by our society.

Long-term memory

In contrast to sensory and short-term memory, long-term memory has an unlimited capacity and its duration can be anything from a few minutes to permanent (Ingleby 2010). This form of memory stores those memories that hold the potential to be retrieved when necessary. The memories located in this 'store' include linguistic memories, conceptual memories and memories of previously learned skills (examples of these previously learned skills can be playing the piano, riding a bike, swimming and so on). All of us disseminate information from short-term memory to long-term memory through 'rehearsal'. We also code information so that it can be placed into relevant categories in our long-term memories. This appears to be similar to sorting out post codes. We all do this, regardless of age. As we have argued, it is the social assumption that older people do not do this that is interesting.

McDougall (1988) supports the argument that the bracketing together of older people and declining memory is a social construction. It is not so much that the memory declines, but more that it becomes harder to retrieve information with age. This has led to research interest in the ways in which information is memorised and subsequently recalled and applied. Brown et al. (2003, p114) consider the processes that operate within the brain and how they affect memories. The three main stages involved with memories are acquisition, storage and retrieval.

Acquisition

In acquiring memories, information must be formed within our memories. Our experiences are placed into our memories. This process is selective – we do not remember every experience, so the research interest considers why certain experiences are retained within the memory. It is important to emphasise that everyone undergoes this process of acquiring memories – this is not a process that is only confined to younger people.

Storage

The storage of memories refers to the information that is contained within the memory. Storage of memories occurs as a result of structural and chemical processes that operate within the brain. We get a 'memory trace' that is either temporary or permanent. A significant part of this process of creating a memory trace involves 'coding' the information which has been attended to in the first instance. 'Chunking' is an example of coding. Again, this is a process that applies to all categories of individuals.

Retrieval

This stage of memory operation involves accessing information that is stored. No matter how attentive we are to our environment and how much of the information within that environment we 'take in', the information is of little use if it cannot be retrieved as and when needed. Retrieval of information from the memory necessitates two techniques: 'recognition' and 'recall'. Recognition involves matching a currently seen item, such as a photograph of a person, with a previous experience of that individual. Recall entails bringing information already stored in the memory into the conscious mind (Ingleby 2010) and involves being able to provide a description of an experience without using prompts or photographs (ibid.).

Draaisma (2004) argues that, in fact, the mind does not deteriorate with age. The coding and storage of information does not necessarily decline: it is more the retrieval of information that becomes an issue. There are, however, cognitive techniques that can be used with older people in order to help with the memory. Poon (1992) argues that as long as older people continue to use strategies for remembering things as they age, their memories will not necessarily experience a significant deterioration. Once more, it is the social perception that older people do not have good memories that needs to change.

REFLECTIVE ACTIVITY 8.10

How can we help older people to become more confident about their memory?

FEEDBACK ON REFLECTIVE ACTIVITY

Interactionist sociologists argue that individuals make sense of the world that they are a part of. We can use this argument to emphasise that older people should not be considered as a separate social category. There are individual older people. Their circumstances are unique and their memories are not necessarily likely to deteriorate. Moreover, if they apply the memory techniques they have used previously, their memories can continue to work effectively. It is important to avoid the self-fulfilling prophecy: if there is an assumption that all older people have poor memories, so older people become like this. It is also important to ensure that this automatic assumption is not reinforced when we are working with older people. The memory is influenced by social factors. Conflict theorists maintain that economic circumstances influence health and well-being, therefore if someone is working in a poorly paid job and has additional social pressures, their memory is likely to be affected whether or not they are an older person.

CONCLUSION

This chapter has explored what sociologists find interesting about older people. We have argued that the concept of age is a social construction, and that different societies at different times have different interpretations of old age. There is not a rigid acceptance of who is old and who is young across societies. In UK society, someone aged 50 years is not necessarily old. If we place that individual in an emerging economy such as Malaysia, they may be regarded as being old because of the young demographic structure of Malaysia. We have reflected on material of interest to medical sociologists. We have explored the changing physical body over time, and we have argued that it is the social interpretation placed on the ageing body that is the most important factor. Old age is a social construction. In our society, there can be a negative portrayal of old age, and we have argued that it is important that this does not become a self-fulfilling prophecy. If there is an assumption that old age results in a deterioration of the body, this may happen due to a belief that this is somehow inevitable. As social workers, it is important to reflect on the interactionist argument that everyone is unique, and to acknowledge that people process the social world in particular ways. The techniques they have used to memorise are still available in old age, but it is the idea that this is somehow not possible that appears to be the issue. It is not necessarily bad that an older person cannot recall everything that has happened to them, and, indeed, this state of mind may be viewed in a positive way. It is possibly a consequence of having had rich and varied experiences that have been so profound that it is not possible to remember everything.

CHAPTER 9

CONCLUSION

SOCIOLOGY AND SOCIAL WORK

This book has explored how sociology can be applied to social work. We have seen that 'sociology' and 'social work' are often referred to in the same sentence. The two areas may be regarded as being allied to each other, but we have seen in the book that sociology is a profound subject area. We have referred to the philosophy that underpins sociological thought. We have argued that the consideration of the social world links back to a number of famous philosophers who enrich our understanding of the nature of the universe. We have seen that social work is a complex profession that is not confined to championing the rights of vulnerable groups in society. In the UK, social work is a profession that includes a number of highly skilled professionals who work with other professionals in education and health in order to meet the needs of a complex range of individuals. Sociology is one of a number of academic disciplines that informs social work practice. We have proposed that sociology can be misinterpreted, and have stressed the importance of recognising the major contribution that sociology can make to the social work profession.

The book has explored how three key sociological theories (functionalism, interactionism and conflict theory) can be applied to key areas of professional practice in social work: with children, older people, the mentally ill and those who have learning disabilities. The book has focused on these particular sociological perspectives because they are regarded as being the essential paradigms in the discipline of sociology. We have argued that functionalists explore the social factors that influence the world we inhabit, and how functionalists are interested in how the social world generates social meaning. Applying this perspective, 'societies' are regarded as being more important than individuals, and a 'macro' approach is taken in understanding the social world. This links functionalism to the questions that were pursued by philosophers such as Plato (Audi 1999). Functionalists are less concerned with individual perceptions and are more like Plato in their pursuit of answers to big questions. There are social workers who are also interested in the answer to fundamental questions. It can be argued that social work is a complex profession that welcomes the pursuit of moral and ethical justice so the profession is more than a collection of individuals. In this example, social forces are regarded as being beyond individuals.

We have seen the influence of a contrasting sociological perspective – interactionism (Ingleby 2013). The book explains that interactionism is based on exploring the perceptions of individuals. As opposed to seeking causes behind social factors that are beyond individuals, the meaning generated by individuals becomes central to the social world. We used the work of Audi (1999) to refer to this perception of the world as being a Copernican revolution of thought. We argued that, in a similar way to Copernicus (who revealed that the universe revolves around the sun), so interactionists emphasise the importance of looking at the social world differently. We have seen that interactionists contend that there is no point in pursuing 'big questions' that we will not get answers to. In exemplifying this point, we argued that, we are unlikely to reveal the fundamental essence of 'love' in its entirety. We can, however, ask an individual how it feels to be loved. In this way, the big question is turned around – it becomes a 'smaller' question that can be answered. In exploring sociology in this way, the perceptions of individuals are revealed. We have seen that key questions such as 'How do you feel?' are being asked by social workers as they work with others. This makes this second sociological perspective so important to the content of the book.

The third sociological model that we have applied in the book is conflict theory. This sociological perspective is based on the philosophy of Marx. In this sociological theory, the consequences of the material world are studied. We have seen that Marx draws attention to the importance of economic forces by considering the impact that the material world has on the lives of individuals. We have also made a connection between conflict theory and functionalism. In classical Marxism, an emphasis is placed on the importance of wider economic forces that are beyond individuals in that they are regarded as transcending the person. Capitalism is an example of an economic system that predates all of us. We have argued that there is a strong possibility that this economic system will exist beyond individuals for many years to come. We have suggested that in classical Marxism, the economy is interpreted in ways that are similar to functionalism. In this sense, the economy is regarded as being greater than individuals. We have also argued that the complexity of conflict theory is revealed through neo-Marxism and its focus on enabling individuals to engage with social structures, so that new understandings of the social world are generated. We have contended that this connects neo-Marxism to interactionism. The thinking, conscious individuals in societies should not be regarded as being distinct from economic forces, but as interacting with the social world by creating meaning in profound ways. We have argued that this way of thinking about the social world connects with much social work practice. As opposed to viewing social factors as the cause of every social problem, there is awareness that individuals are also influential as they engage in creating a social world that is meaningful. We have proposed that conflict theory is a useful sociological concept because it embraces both strands of sociological thought. This appears to be a sensible way of resolving what seems to be an either/or dilemma, and, in turn, enables us to find appropriate ways of dealing with the issues that are presented to us as social workers. The advantage of this approach is such that it enables us to apply sociological explanations to social work that are based on a combination of individual and social factors.

HOLISTIC PRACTICE

This book reveals the importance of holistic practice when we are working as social workers. In applying holistic practice to social work, we are basing our professional work on being open to new ideas. We are accepting that we can change and that those we work with have the capacity to change too through embracing new concepts. The book adopts this philosophy of holistic practice by considering theories from sociology in unison. The theories are not separated and confined to academic debates in this book. The sociological theories that we have reflected on link to all aspects of our work with key groups in social work. It is interesting to consider how these sociological theories inform our work in the field. In applying this holistic practice, it is important for us to ensure that we combine ideas together so that there is a flexible approach that is being adopted in our professional practice. This is a key theme of the book.

In considering this concept of holistic practice, it is also important to reflect on other subject areas that link to sociology. There are ideas within psychology that are also connected to sociology and if we are also aware of the ideas of key psychological theories and we combine these ideas with sociological theories, we can enhance our practice even more. This is likely to make our professional work holistic. In psychology, as in sociology, there is much interest in the relationship that exists between individuals and social structures. We have argued that functionalists and conflict theorists are interested in forces that are beyond individuals. This is linked to the thinking of philosophers, including Plato, who reflect on the nature of forces that are beyond individual human beings. In psychology, behaviourism explores the influence of the environment on individual human beings. Once again, what is beyond the individual is being considered in this strand of psychology. If we are able see the connections that exist between functionalism, conflict theory and behaviourism, this will in turn enhance our professional practice as we can blend the ideas together to enrich our work in the field.

Linking functionalism, conflict theory and behaviourism together is an example of holistic theorising. We are making connections and links together between theories that are often thought about in separate subject disciplines. We are essentially breaking through traditional academic boundaries when we combine ideas together in this way. If we are able to combine the academic ideas together from different disciplines when we are working with varied groups of individuals in social work, this is a further example of holistic thinking. Hopefully the book will encourage you to think about combining sets of ideas from academic disciplines together as you are working as a social worker. If we reflect on how functionalism and conflict theory can help us in our social work practice alongside considering the important contribution that is being made by allied subject areas such as psychology, this provides us with an opportunity to demonstrate this excellent professional practice.

In the book, we have seen that interactionist sociologists are interested in individuals and their unique understanding of the world. We have argued that this connects interactionism to the philosophy of Immanuel Kant and the pursuit of understanding how 'phenomena' are generated by individuals. The interest in individuals is also apparent in other academic subject areas in the social sciences. In psychology, the interest in individual interpretations of the world is central to the work of humanist psychologists including Carl Rogers and Abraham Maslow (Ingleby 2013). Both of these psychologists focus on the importance of individual interpretations of the social world. If we are able to make connections between interactionism and the work of humanist psychologists, we are once more demonstrating holistic practice. We are combining sets of ideas together that are traditionally associated with belonging to particular subject disciplines.

The social work profession in the UK is a graduate-led profession. This reveals the wish to have professionals who are highly educated and able to make a difference to the lives of others. It is through becoming aware of holistic practice that this excellent professional practice is more likely to happen. Upon thinking in innovative and different ways, we are more likely to witness holistic practice. We are seeking to combine sets of ideas so that there is an enabling of innovative thinking in order to blend theories together. This then allows us to challenge 'fixed ways of thinking'.

This different way of thinking about the social world is not new. There are examples of thinkers in the past who have urged us to adopt a new way of viewing the social world. In the book we have made reference to the French philosopher Maurice Blondel. In Blondel's (1893) work, he recommends that individuals ought to adopt a sense of 'action' that enables them to be true to their own beliefs alongside working with established social structures. Blondel was interested in how 'dogma' and 'beliefs' that come from social organisations can be enabled to realise individual potential. In some respects Blondel's (1893) work links to the tension that can appear between interactionism and functionalism and conflict theory. As opposed to placing an emphasis that weighs too heavily on either 'the state' or 'the individual', it is important to enable a sense of balance. This recommendation is also at the heart of holistic practice. We do not become convinced of the absolute merits of one form of thought. We are, instead open to flexible ways of thinking that explore the merits of particular theories. In the book we argue that this blending together of functionalist, interactionist and conflict theorist understandings of the world empowers us during our professional practice as social workers. This is the basis of using sociology and other disciplines in order to evidence holistic practice.

FINAL COMMENTS

There can be an interpretation of sociology and social work that is not positive. Sociology may be viewed as a subject area that is radical and too challenging to conventions that are regarded as being acceptable. Social work may be seen as an 'impossible' profession because the needs of individuals who are so complex can never be met. Both of these views are not helpful. We have seen that sociology is a rich academic discipline that deals with some of the most interesting debates that have ever concerned humanity. Why are we who we are? There could not be a more interesting question to pursue. We have argued that the individuals we are working with in the field are formed as a consequence of a combination of factors. Some of these factors are individual and particular, but other factors are social and material. Sociology can provide answers to many of the questions that we ask as we approach our work in the field. When I worked in social work I would ask myself why the individuals I encountered were so needy. Was it because 'this is just the way it is' or have social factors moulded these individuals in profound ways? Sociology gives us key answers to these questions. Moreover, social work is a fine profession. Those who are working as social workers are attempting to influence the physical, intellectual, emotional and social development of all those that they are working with. The challenges in the profession can be significant as the complexity of those we are working with as social workers can be immense. If, however, we do make a positive difference to the lives of those we are working with, we have fulfilled our professional objectives and sociology is a subject that can help us to realise this goal.

REFERENCES

Allbrow, M. 1970. *Bureaucracy*. London: Macmillan.

Anderson, M. 1980. *Approaches to the History of the Western Family 1500–1914*. London: Macmillan.

Atkinson, R.L., R.C. Atkinson, E.E. Smith and E.R. Hilgard. 1987. *Psychology*. Sydney: Harcourt Brace Jovanovich.

Audi, R. 1999. *The Cambridge Dictionary of Philosophy*. Cambridge: Cambridge University Press.

Ballard, R. 1990. Marriage and Family in C. Clarke, C. Peach and S. Vertovec (eds) *South Asians Overseas*. Cambridge: Cambridge University Press.

Bandura, A. 1977. *Social Learning Theory*. London: Prentice Hall.

Bateson, G. 1972. *Steps to an Ecology of Mind: Collected Essays in Anthropology, Psychiatry, Evolution and Epistemology*. Chicago IL: University of Chicago Press.

Baudrillard, J. 1983a. *Simulations*. London: MIT Press.

Baudrillard, J. 1983b. *Symbolic Exchange and Death*. London: Sage.

Berger, P. 1983. *The War Over the Family*. London: Hutchinson.

Bernard, M., J. Phillips, Machin, L. Machin and V. Harding Davies. 2000. *Women Ageing: Changing Identities, Challenging Myths*. London: Routledge.

Biebel, D.B. and H.G. Koenig. 2004. *New Light on Depression: Help, Hope and Answers for the Depressed and Those Who Love Them*. Grand Rapidsh MI: Zondervan.

Blondel, M. 1893. *Action (1893): Essay on a Critique of Life and a Science of Practice*. Paris: University of Notre Dame Press.

Booth, T. and M. Ainscow. 2002. *Index for Inclusion: Developing Learning and Participation in Schools*. London: Centre for Studies on Inclusive Education.

Bourdieu, P. 1986. *Questions de Sociologique*. Paris: Les Éditions de Minuit.

Bourdieu, P. 1993. *Outline of a Theory of Practice*. Cambridge: Cambridge University Press.

Brown, A., R. Cocking and J. Bransford. 2003. *How People Learn: Brain, Mind, Experience and School*. Washington DC: National Academy Press.

Casey, T. 2010. *Inclusive Play: Practical Strategies for Children from Birth to Eight*, 2nd ed. London: Sage.

Cashmere, E.E. 1985. *United Kingdom?* London: Unwin Hyman.

Chandler, J. 1991. *Women without Husbands: An Exploration of the Margins of Marriage*. London: Macmillan.

Chester, R. 1985. The Rise of the Neo-Conventional Family. *New Society*, 9 May.

Cheston, R. and M. Bender. 2003. *Understanding Dementia: The Man with the Worried Eyes*. London: Jessica Kingsley.

Coffield, F., D. Moseley, E. Hall and K. Ecclestone. 2004. *Learning Styles and Pedagogy in Post-16 Learning: A Systematic and Critical Review*. London: Learning and Skills Development Agency (LSDA).

Davis, K. 1948. *Human Society*. New York: Macmillan.

Devarakonda, C. 2013. *Diversity and Inclusion in Early Childhood*. London: Sage.

Department for Education (DfE) 2017. *Statutory Framework for the Early Years Foundation Stage*. London: DfE.

Department for Education and Employeement (DfEE) 1997. *Excellence for All Children: Meeting Special Educational Needs*. London: DfEE.

Downie, R. 2000. *The Healing Arts*. Oxfod: Oxford University Press.

Draaisma, D. 2004. *Why Life Speeds Up as You Get Older*. Cambridge: Cambridge University Press.

Durkheim, E. 1893/1984. *The Division of Labour in Society*. Basingstoke: Macmillan.

Durkheim, E. 1899–1900. The Two Laws of Penal Evolution in *L'annee sociologique*, Vol. 4. 65–95, 1899–1900. In M. Traugott (ed. and trans.) (1978) *Emile Durkheim on Institutional Analysis*. Chicago IL and London: University of Chicago Press.

Durkheim, E. 2002. *Moral Education*. New York: Dover Publications.

Early Years Foundation Stage (EYFS) (n.d). Available at: https://www.gov.uk/early-years-foundation-stage#content (accessed 28 June 2017).

Education (Handicapped Children) Act. 1970. London: Her Majesty's Stationery Office. (HMSO)

Education Act. 1981. London: HMSO.

Education Act. 1993. London: HMSO.

Education Act. 1996. London: HMSO.

Ellingson, L.L. 2009. *Engaging Crystallization in Qualitative Research*. London: Sage.

Every Child Matters. 2003. Norwich: The Stationery Office.

Fitzgerald, D. 2004. *Parent Partnership in the Early Years*. London: Continuum.

Forgacs, D. 2014. *The Antonio Gramsci Reader: Selected Writings 1916–1935*. London: Aakar Books.

Golightley, M. 2004. *Social Work and Mental Health*. Exeter: Learning Matters.

Gottesman, I.I. and J. Shields. 1982. *Schizophrenia: The Epigenetic Puzzle*. New York: Cambridge University Press.

Gough, K. 1959. Nayar Central Kerela in D. Schneider and K. Gough (eds) *Matrilineal Kinship*. Cambridge: Cambridge University Press.

Grey-Davidson, F. 1999. *The Alzheimer's Sourcebook for Caregivers*. Chicago IL: Lowell House.

Habermas, J. 1981. *The Theory of Communicative Action*. London: Heinemann.

Hannerz, U. 1991. *Cultural Complexity: Studies in the Social Organisation of Meaning*. New York: Columbia University Press.

Haralambos, M. and M. Holborn. 2008. *Sociology: Themes and Perspectives*. London: HarperCollins.

Hart, N. 1976. *When Marriage Ends: A Study in Status Passage*. London: Tavistock Press.

Hirst, P.Q. and P. Woolley. 1982. *Social Relations and Human Attributes*. London: Tavistock.

Hobbes, T. 1651/1962. *Leviathan*. London: Collins.

Holliday, R. 1995. *Understanding Ageing*. Cambridge: Cambridge University Press.

Holmes, T. and R. Rahe. 1967. The Social Readjustment Scale. *Journal of Psychosomatic Research* 1 (1): 213–18.

Horn, J.L. and G. Donaldson. 1976. On the Myth of Intellectual Decline in Adulthood. *American Psychologist* 30 (1): 701–19.

Horn, J.L., and G. Donaldson. 1977. Faith is Not Enough: A Response to the Baltes-Schaie Claim that Intelligence Does Not Wane. *American Psychologist* 32: (1): 369–73.

Ingleby, E. 2010. *Applied Psychology for Social Work*, 2nd ed. Exeter: Learning Matters.

Ingleby, E. 2013. *Early Childhood Studies: A Social Science Perspective*. London: Bloomsbury.

Ingleby, E., G. Oliver and R. Winstone. 2014. *Early Childhood Studies: Enhancing Employability and Professional Practice*. London: Bloomsbury.

James, W. 1995. *Immunisation: The Reality behind the Myth*. Westport CT: Greenwood Press.

Johnson, M. 2005. *The Cambridge Book of Ageing*. Cambridge: Cambridge University Press.

Kesey, K. 1962. *One Flew Over the Cuckoo's Nest*. London: Picador.

Klatz, R. and R. Goldman. 1997. *Stopping the Clock*. New Caanan CT: Keats Publishing.

Laslett, P. 1972. *Household and Family in Past Time*. Cambridge: Cambridge University Press.

Leach, E. 1997. *A Runaway World*. London: BBC Publications.

Lewis, I.M. 1981. *Social Anthropology in Perspective*. London: Penguin Books.

Lopez, J. and J. Scott. 2000. *Social Structure*. Buckingham: Open University Press.

Lord, S., C. Sherrington and H. Menz. 1994. *Falls in Older People: Risk Factors and Strategies for Prevention*. Cambridge: Cambridge University Press.

Marx, K. 2013. *Capital: Volumes One and Two* (Classics of World Literature). London: Wordsworth Editions.

McDougall, G.J. 1998. Memory Awareness in Nuring Home Residents. *Gerontology* 44 (1): 281–7.

McLellan, D. 1986. *Marx*. London: Fontana.

Metchnikoff, E. 2000. *The Evolutionary Papers of Ellie Metchnikoff*. Dordrecht: Kluwer Academic Publishers.

Miller, G.A. 1956. The Magic Number Seven Plus One or Minus Two: Some Limits to Our Capacity for Processing Information. *Psychological Review* 63 (1): 81–97.

Morgan, D. 1986. Gender in R. Burgess (ed.) *Key Variables in Social Integration*. London: Routledge and Kegan Paul.

Murdock, G.P. 1949. *Social Structure*. New York: Macmillan Press.

Nutbrown, C., P. Gough and F. Atherton. 2013. *Inclusion in the Early Years*, 2nd ed. London: Sage.

Office for National Statistics (ONS). Available at: www.ons.gov.uk/ (Accessed 30 June 2017).

Office for Standards in Education (Ofsted). 2000. *Evaluating Educational Inclusion: Guidance for Inspectors and Schools*. London: HMSO.

Orwell, G. 2013. *Animal Farm*. London: Maple Press.

Parsons, T. 1967. *The Structure of Social Action*. New York: Free Press.

Parton, N. 2005. *Safeguarding Children: Early Intervention and Surveillance in Late Modern Society*. London: Palgrave Macmillan.

Piaget, J. 1962. *Language and Thought of The Child*. London: Routledge.

Plath, S. 1963. *The Bell Jar*. London: Faber and Faber.

Poon, L.W., D. Rubin and B. Wilson. 1992. *Everyday Cognition in Adulthood and Later Life*. Cambridge: Cambridge University Press.

Rapoport, R.N., M.P. Fogarty and R. Rapoport. 1982. *Families in Britain*. London: Kegan Paul.

Rogers, C. 2004. *On Becoming a Person*. London: Robinson.

Salamanaca Statement and Framework for Action on Special Needs Education. 1994. Salamanaca: United Nations Educational, Scientific and Cultural Education (UNESCO).

Saunders, A.R. and P.V. Gejman. 2001. Influential Ideas and Experimental Progress in Schizophrenia Genetics Research. *Journal of the American Medical Association* 285 (1): 2831–3.

Schaie, K.W. 1996. *Intellectual Development in Adulthood: The Seattle Longitudinal Study*. Cambridge: Cambridge University Press.

Special Educational Needs and Disability Act. 2001. London: HMSO.

Sprenger, M. 1999. *Learning and Memory: The Brain in Action*. Rosewood MA: Association for Supervision and Curriculum Development.

Starr, B., and M. Weiner. 1981. *The Starr-Weiner Report on Sex and Sexuality in Mature Years*. New York: McGraw-Hill.

Steele, J.G., E. Treasure, N.B. Pitts, J. Morris and G. Bradnock. 1998. Total Tooth Loss in the UK in 1998 and the Implications for the Future. *British Dental Journal* 189 (11): 598–603.

Taylor, P., J. Richardson, A. Yeo, I. Marsh, K. Trobe and A. Pilkington. 2004. *Sociology in Focus*. Ormskirk: Causeway Press.

Tedam, P. 2009. Understanding Diversity in T. Waller (ed.) *An Introduction to Early Childhood*, 2nd ed. London: Sage.

United Nations (UN).1989. *United Nations Convention on the Rights of the Child*. London: Unicef.

United Nations Children's Fund (UNICEF), A Summary of the UN Convention on the Rights of the Child. Available at: https://downloads.unicef.org.uk/wp-content/uploads/2010/05/UNCRC_summary.pdf (accessed 2 May 2017).

Urban, M. 2009. Strategies for Change: Rethinking Professional Development to Meet the Challenges of Diversity in the Early Years Profession. Paper presented at the International Professional Development Association (IPDA) Conference, 27–28 November, Birmingham, UK.

Vakil, S., R. Freeman and T.J. Swim. 2003. The Reggio Emilia Approach and Inclusive Early Childhood Programs. *Early Childhood Education Journal* 30 (3): 187–92.

Vygotsky, L.S. 1978. *Mind in Society: The Development of Higher Psychological Processes*. Cambridge, MA: Harvard University Press.

Warnock, M. 1978. *Report of the Committee of Enquiry into the Education of Handicapped Children and Young People* (Warknock Report). London: HMSO.

Warnoock, M. 2010. *Special Educational Needs: A New Look (Key Debates in Educational Policy)*. London: Bloomsbury.

Weber, M. 1968. *Economy and Society: An Outline of Interpretive Sociology*. New York: Bedminster Press.

Whitehead, P. 2010. Social Theory and Probation: Exploring Organisational Complexity within a Modernising Context. *Social and Public Policy Review* 4 (2): 15–33.

Wynne, L.C., M.T. Singer, J. Bartko and M.L. Toohey. 1977. Schizophrenics and Their Families: Research on Parental Communication in J.M. Tanner (ed.) *Developments in Psychiatric Research*. London: Hodder and Stoughton.

Zedner, L. 2004. *Criminal Justice*. Oxford: Oxford University Press.

INDEX